A special request please!

A simple review on Amazon really helps me out! If you can, take some time to leave one for me.
You're amazing,
thank you!

Let's connect!

trippy composition

trippy composition

trippy composition

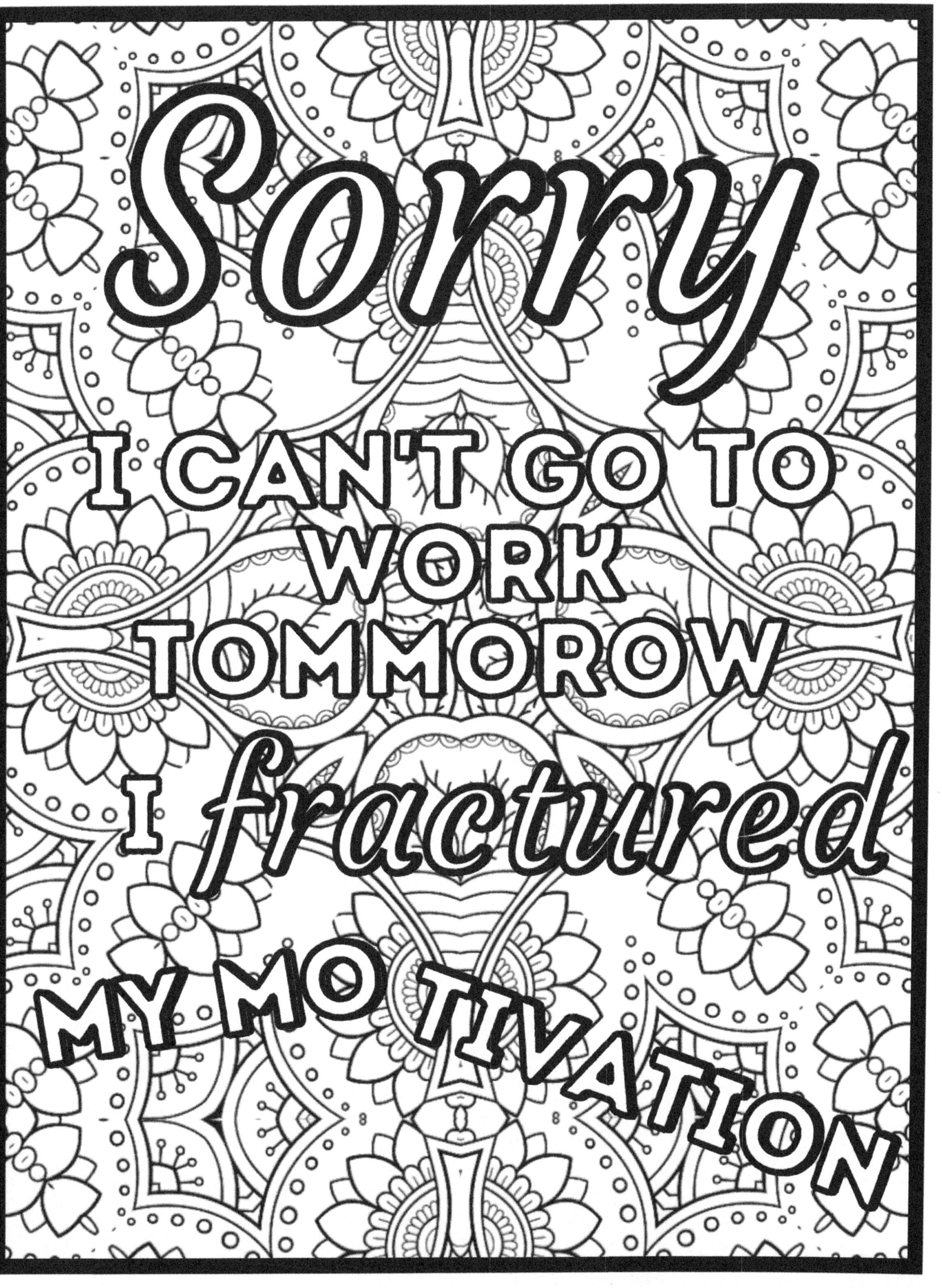
Sorry
I CAN'T GO TO
WORK
TOMMOROW
I fractured
MY MOTIVATION

THE PATH TO *inner peace* BEGINS WITH FOUR WORDS... NOT MY *fucking* PROBLEM

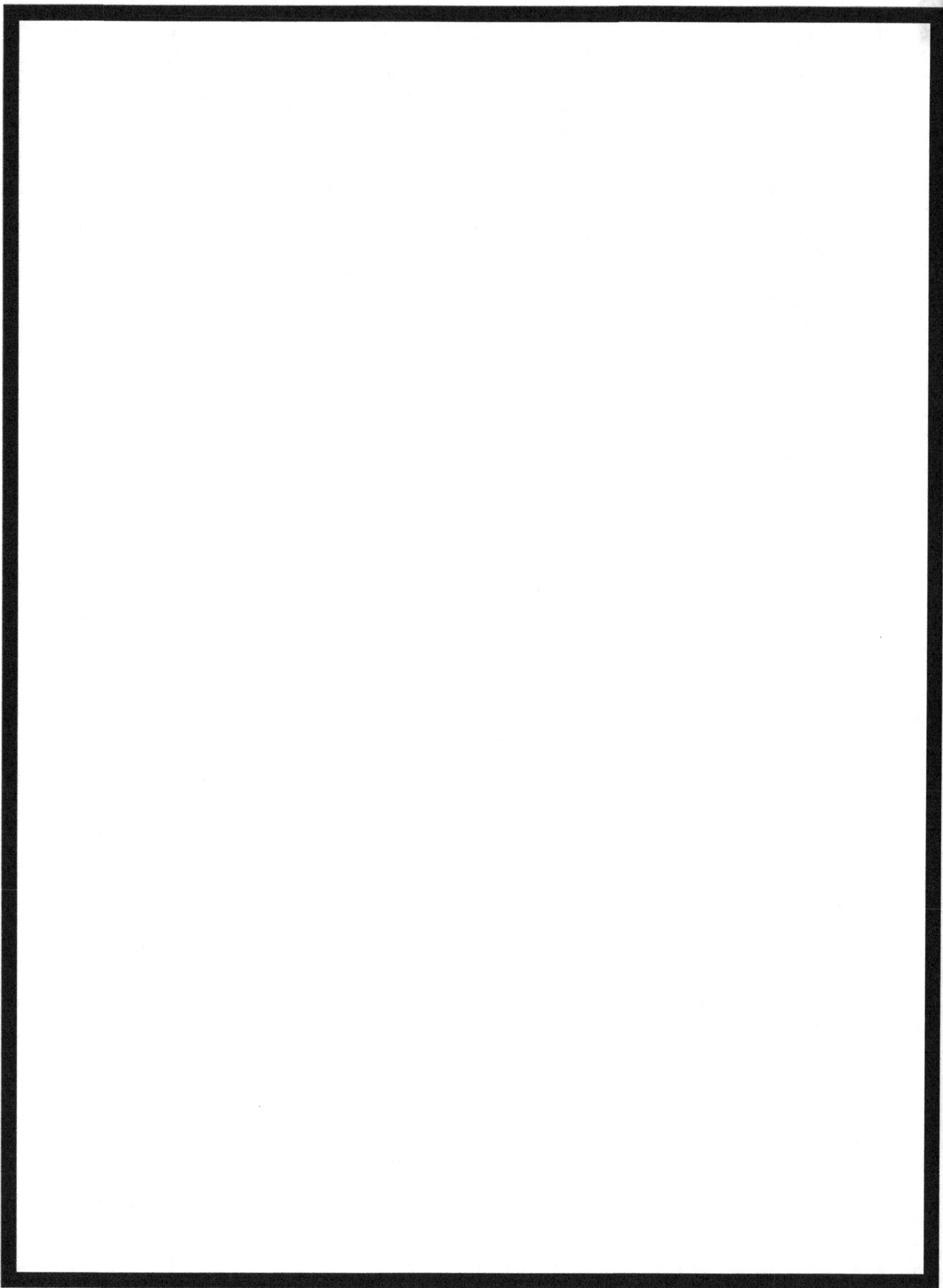

We wanted to be adults **SOOO** baaad.... now look at us, just look

The only person I trust is *me,* and that's even pretty iffy sometimes...

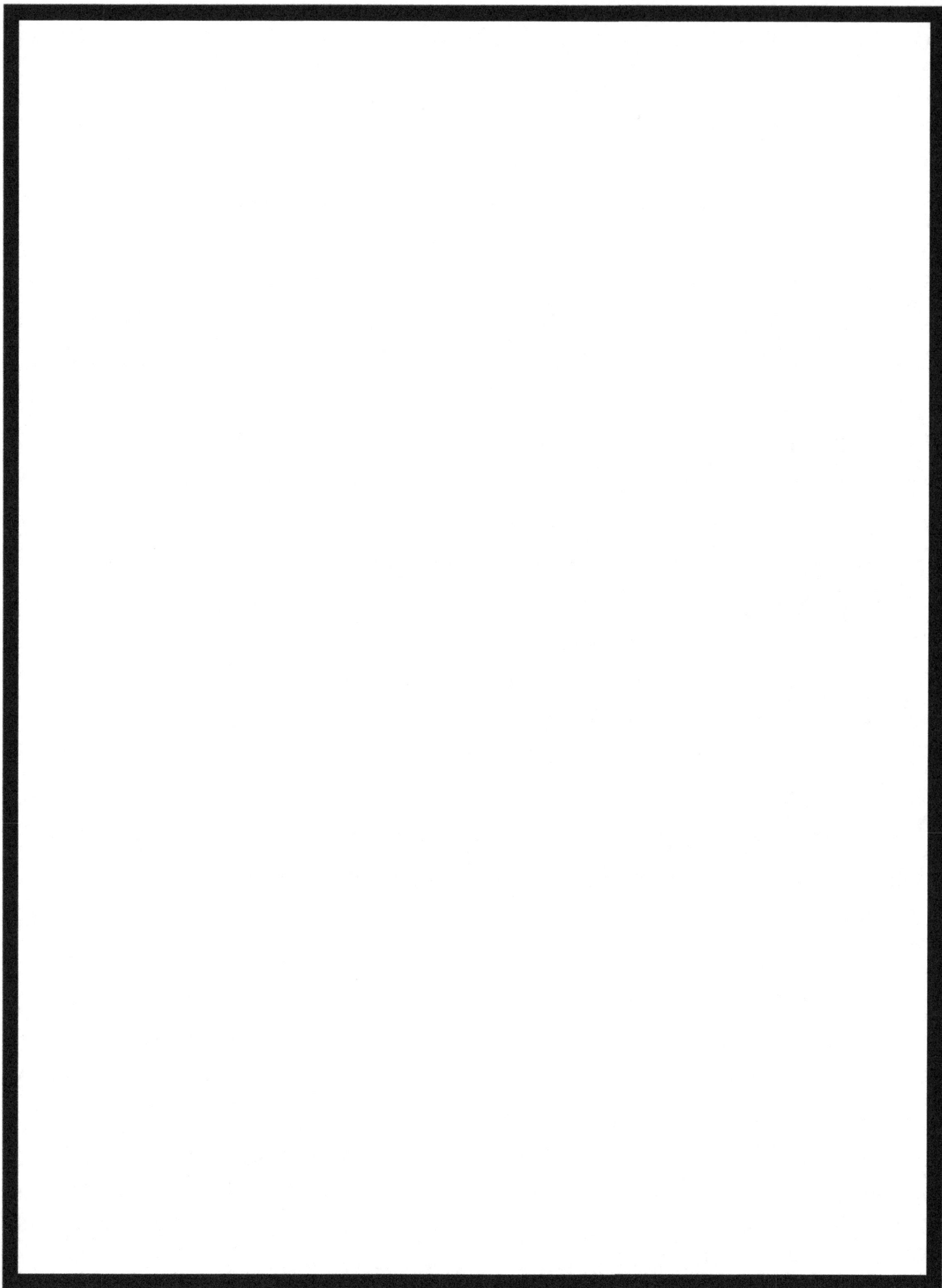

Just because I'm smiling, doesn't mean I don't want to punch you in the face!

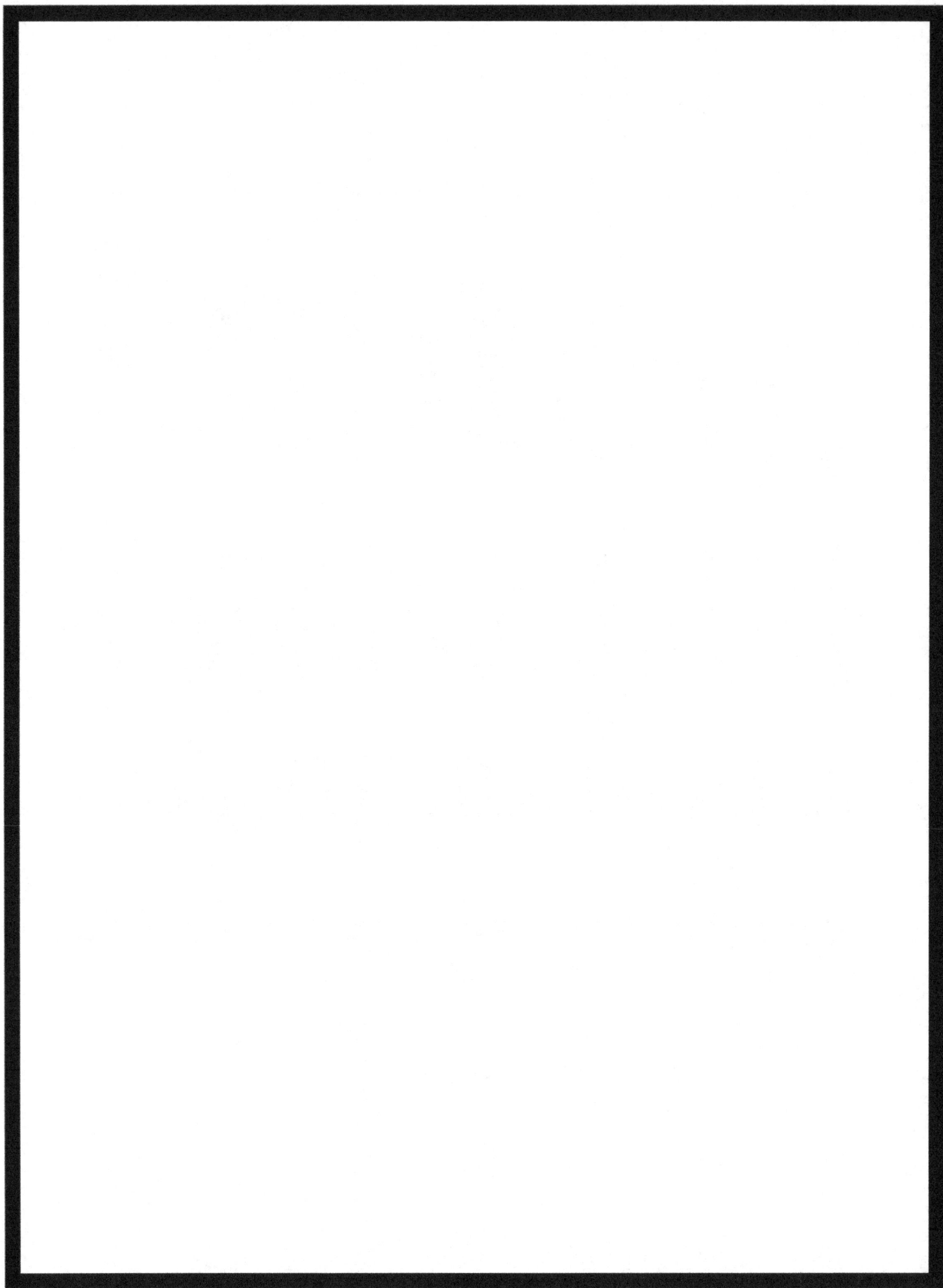

I wish my *life* had background *music* so I could understand what the hell is going on

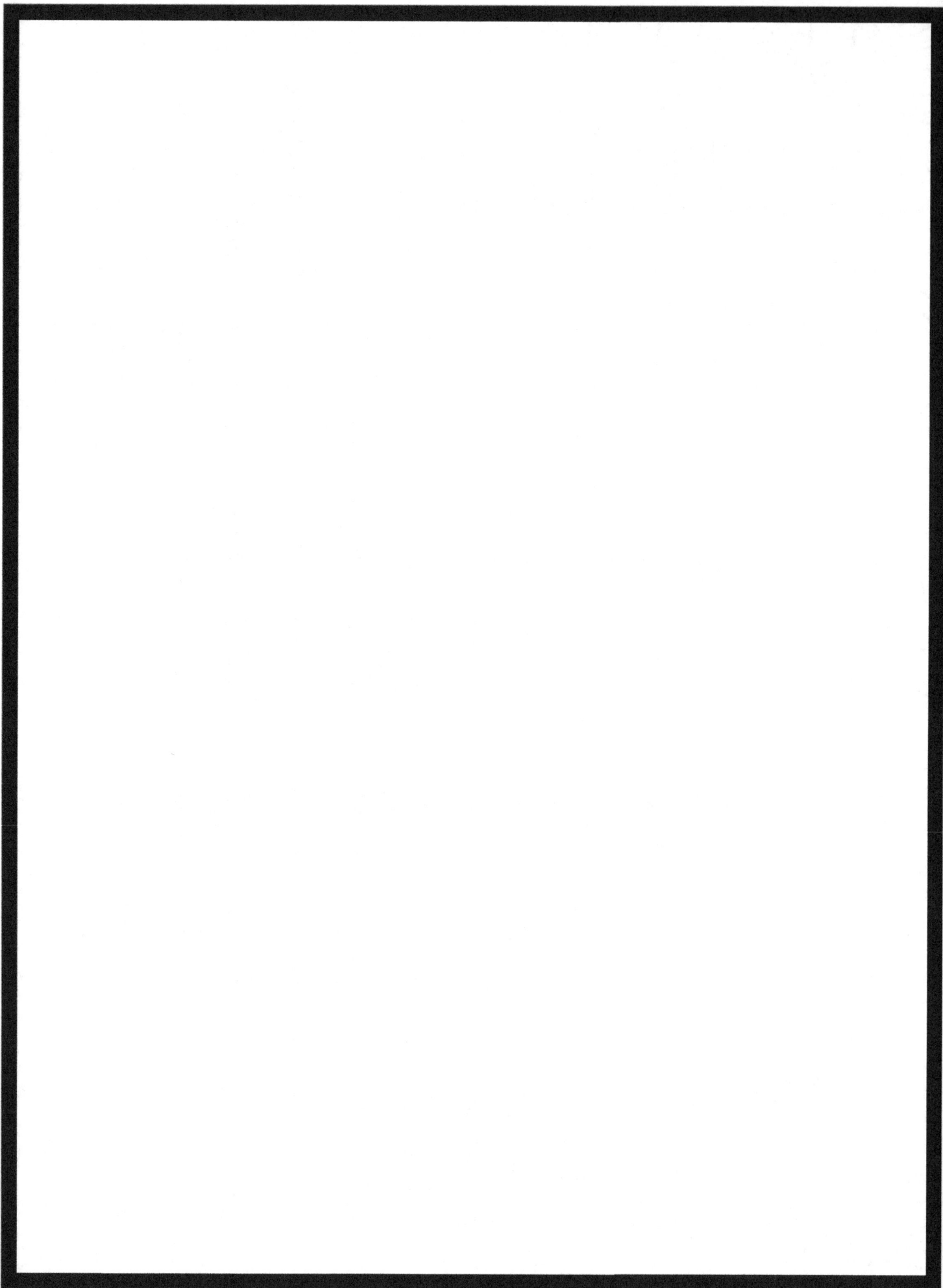

I see your silent treatment and I raise you a FUCK OFF

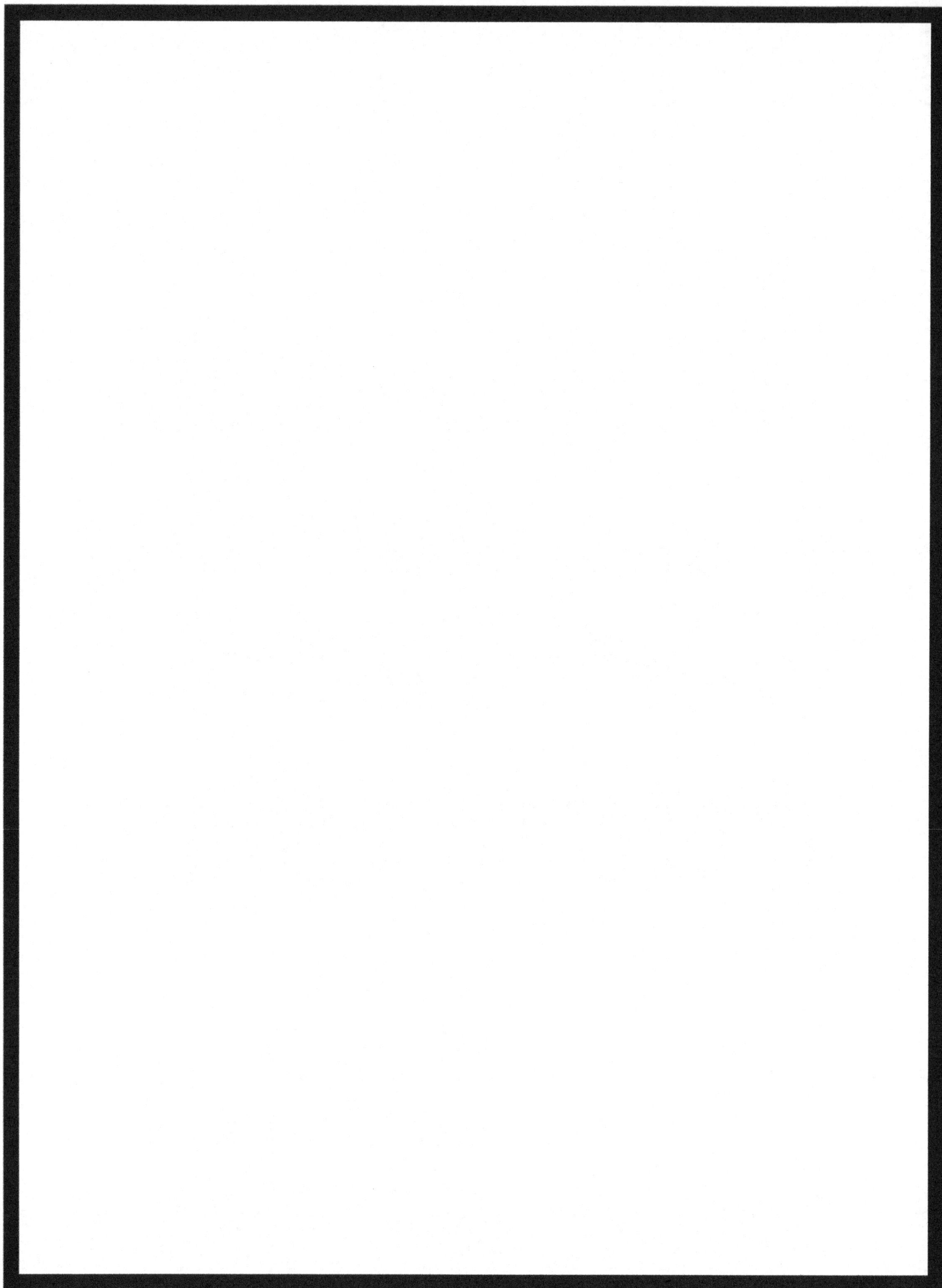

TRY NOT TO BE A TWATSICLE

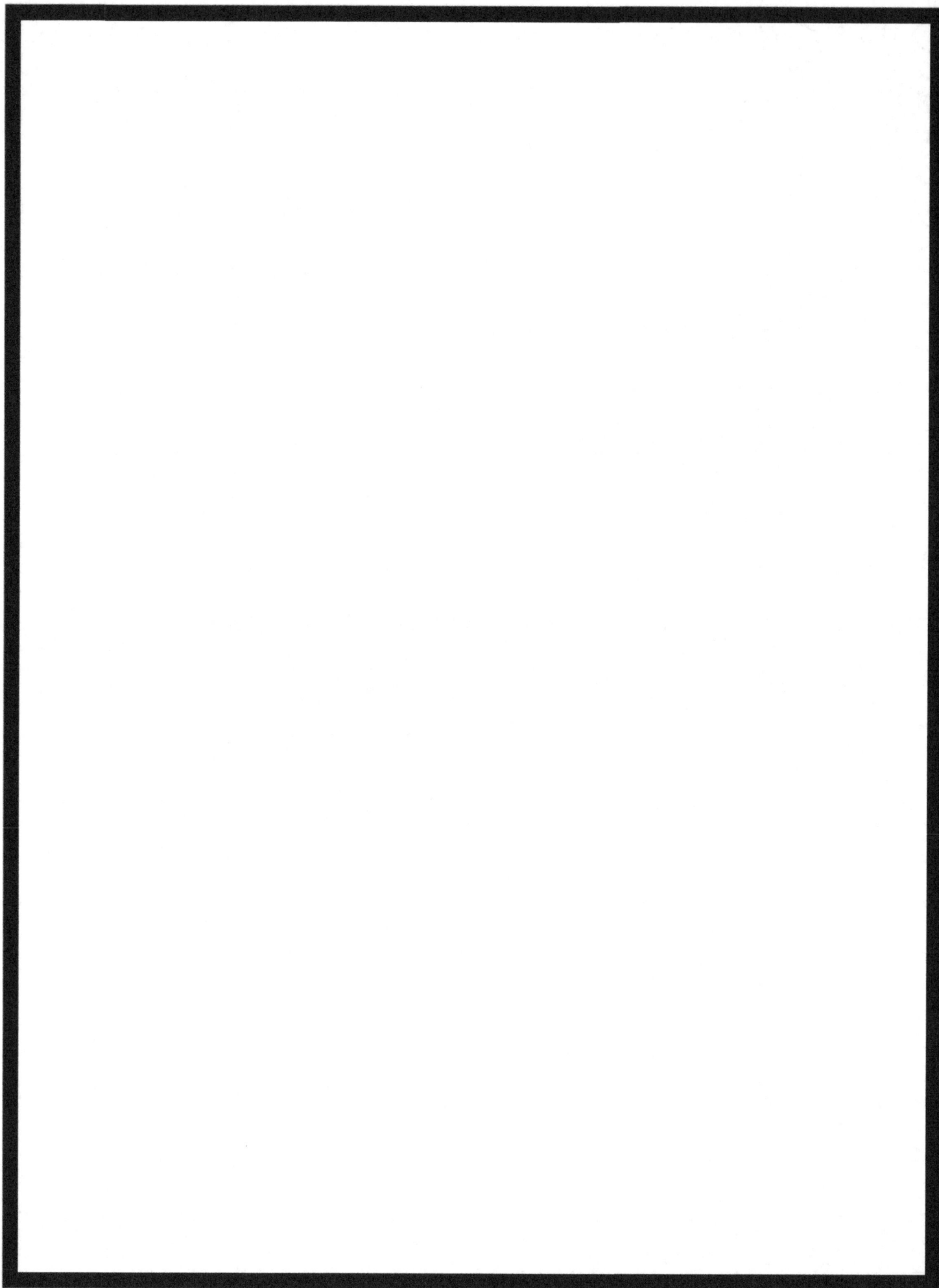

I'M NOT THE TYPE OF PERSON YOU SHOULD PUT ON SPEAKER PHONE

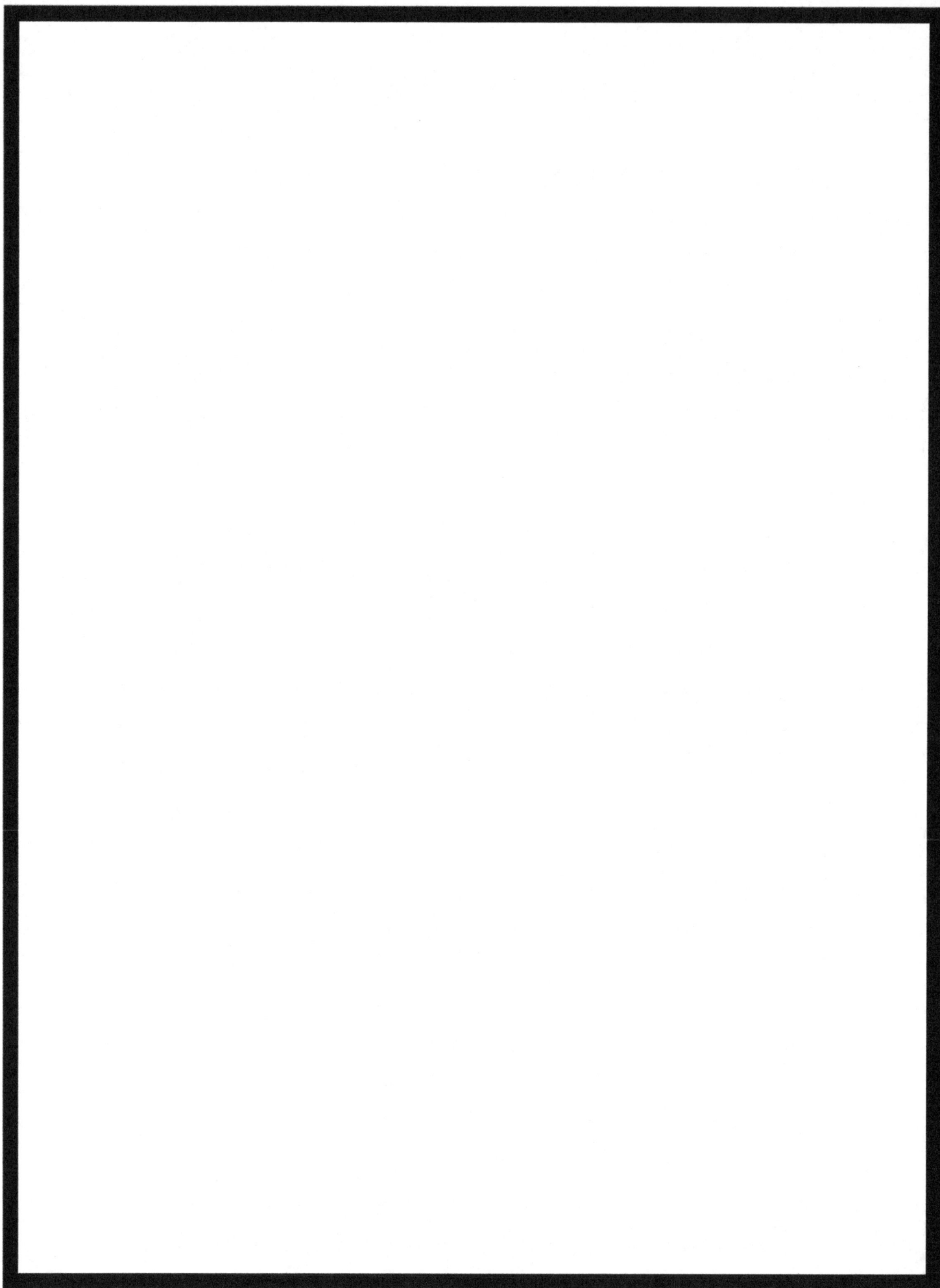

Sometimes I have to tell myself it's just not worth the jail time..

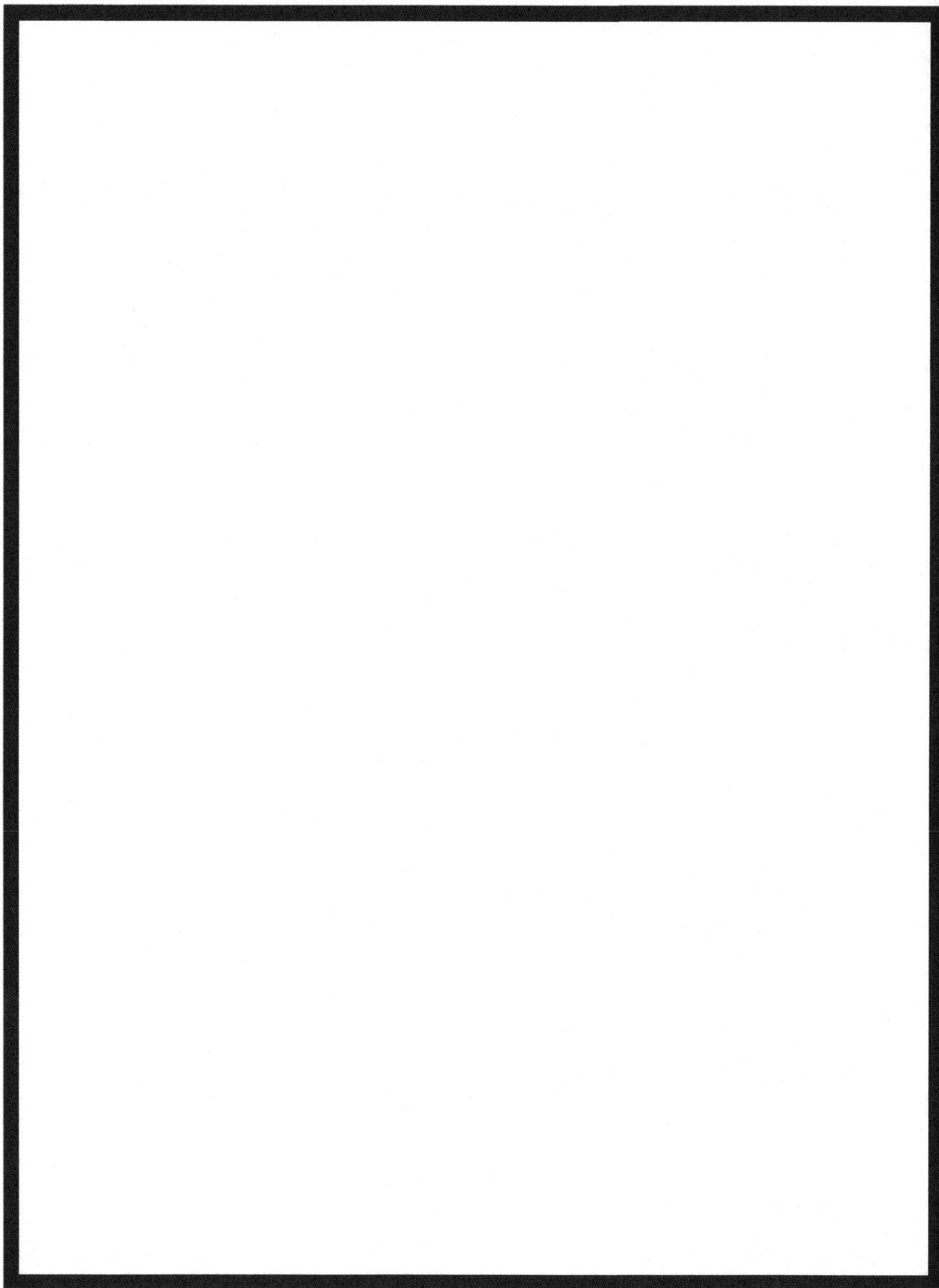

FUCK OFF.
I MEAN *good morning.*

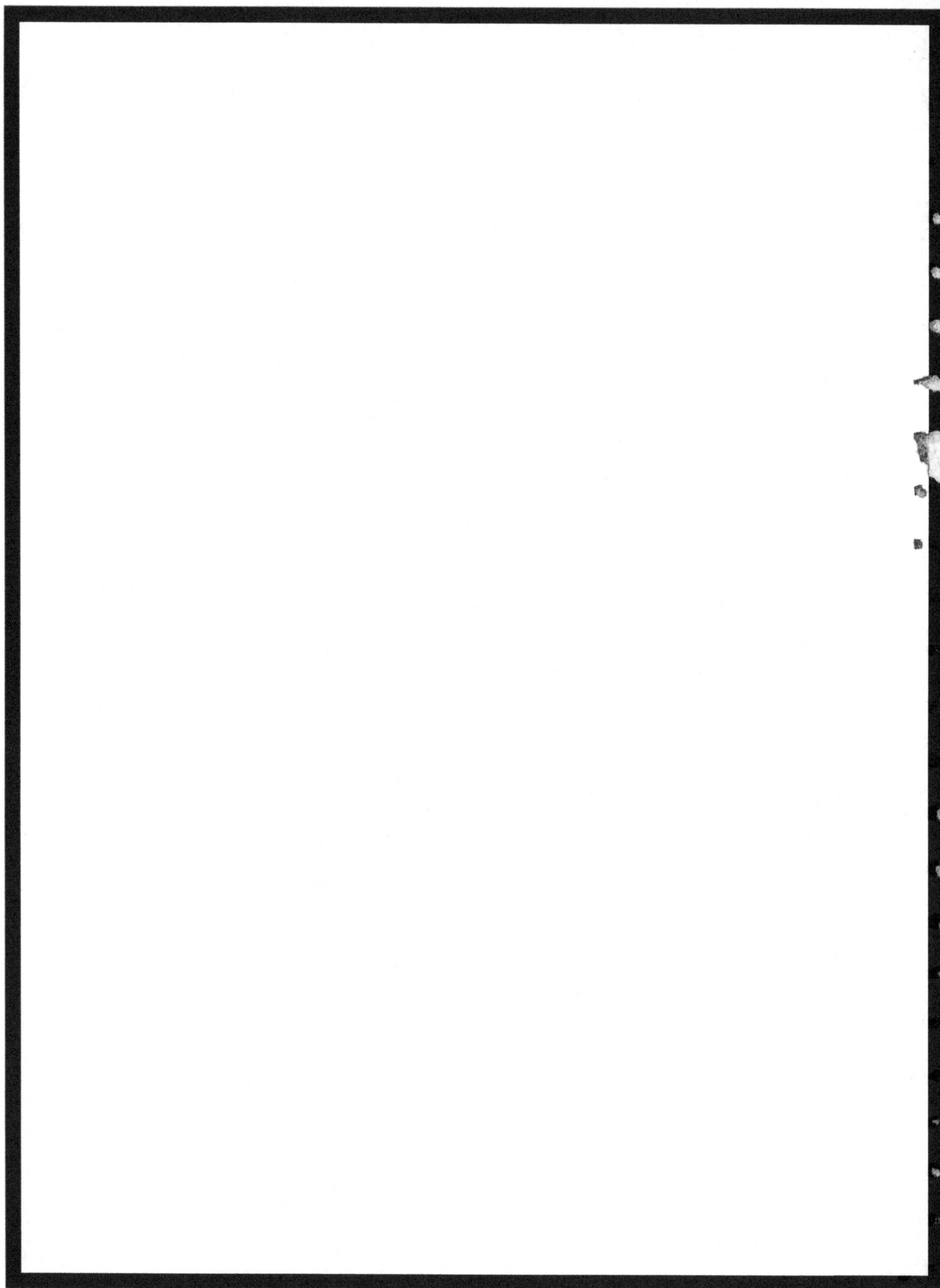

I KNOW, I KNOW I STOOD UP FOR MYSELF, I'M SUCH A BITCH

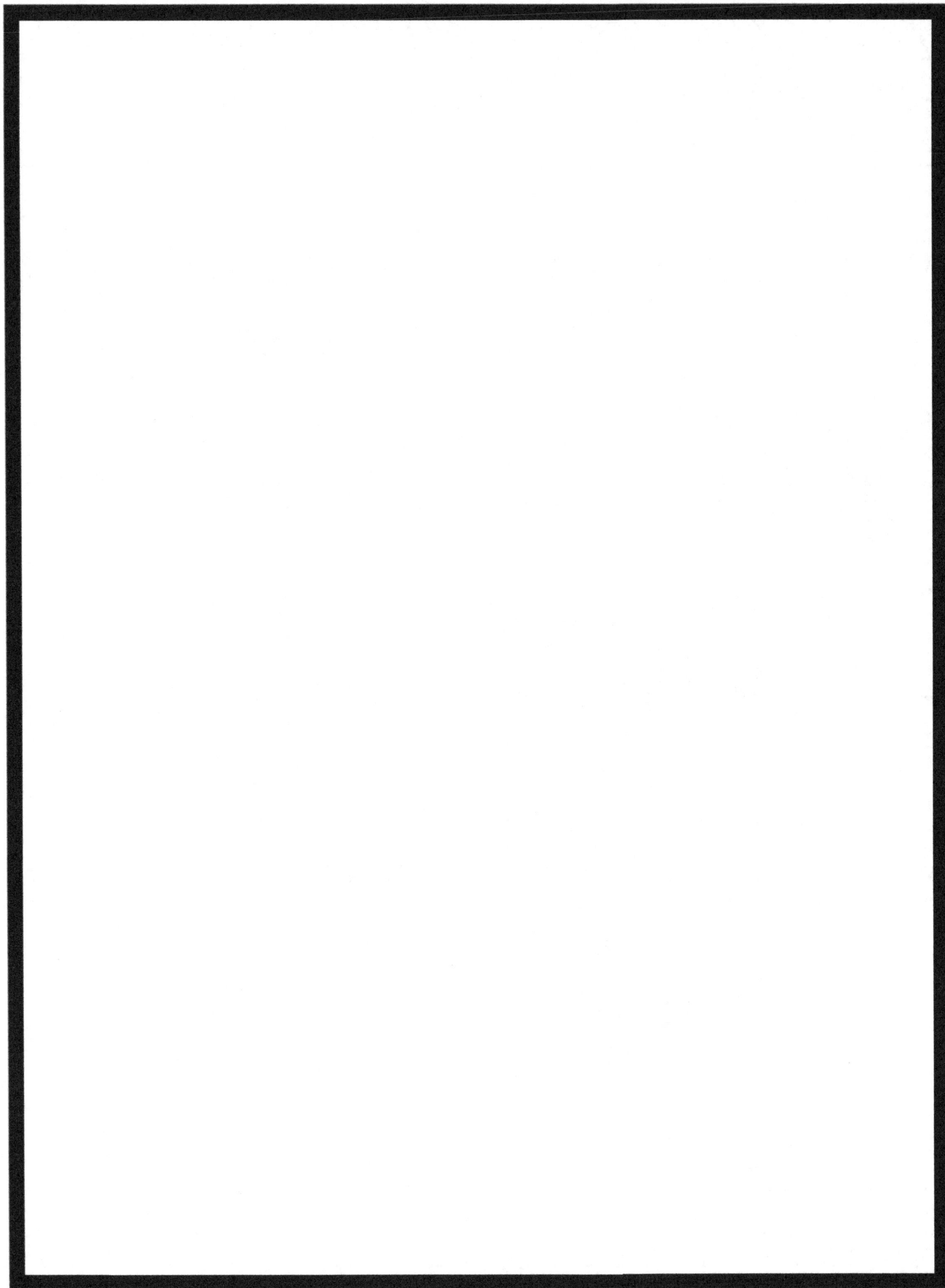

PEOPLE NEED TO START APPRECIATING THE EFFORT I PUT IN TO *NOT* BE A SERIAL KILLER

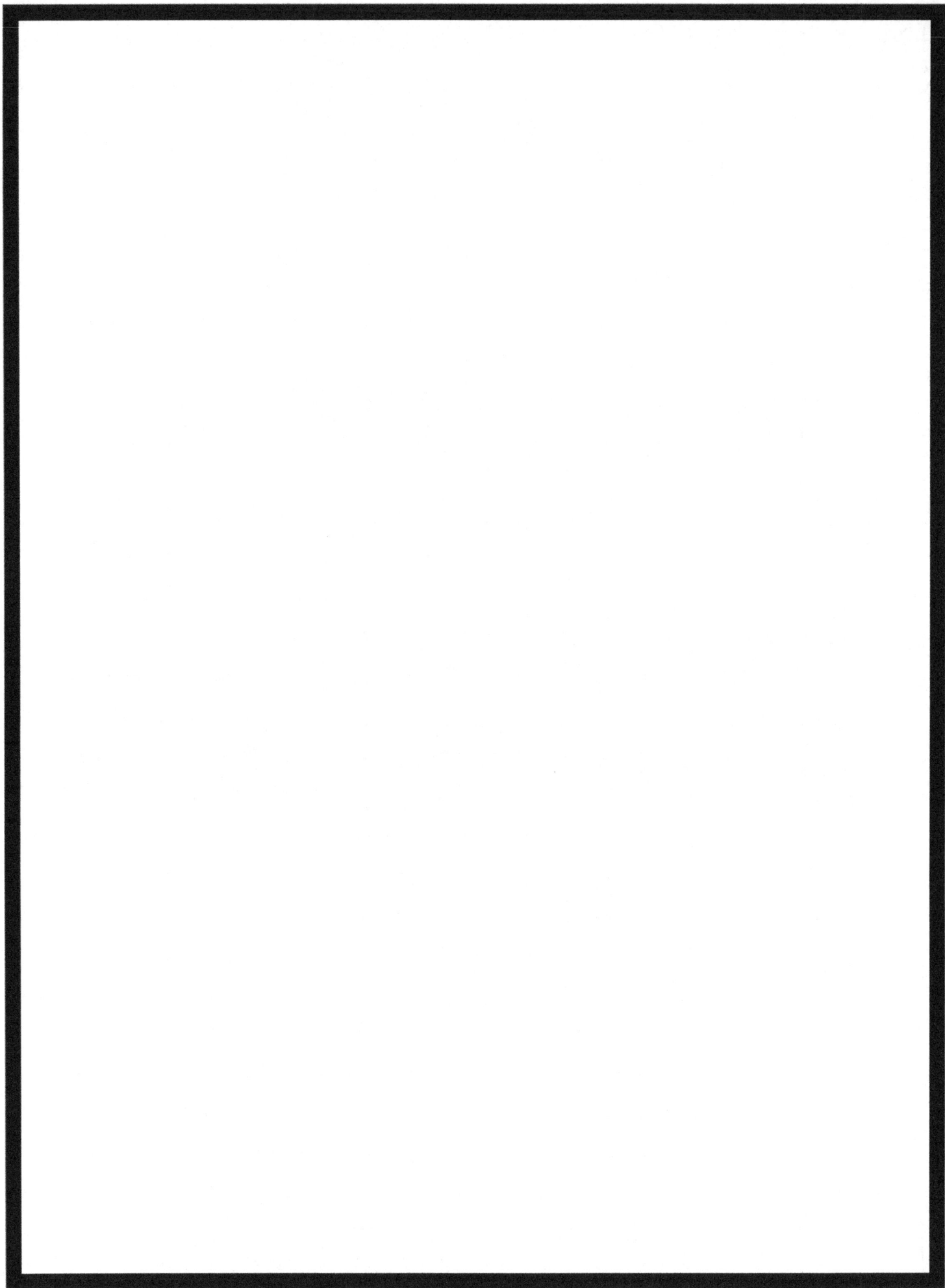

WHOEVER DISCOVERED MILK WAS DOING SOME WEIRD SHIT TO A COW

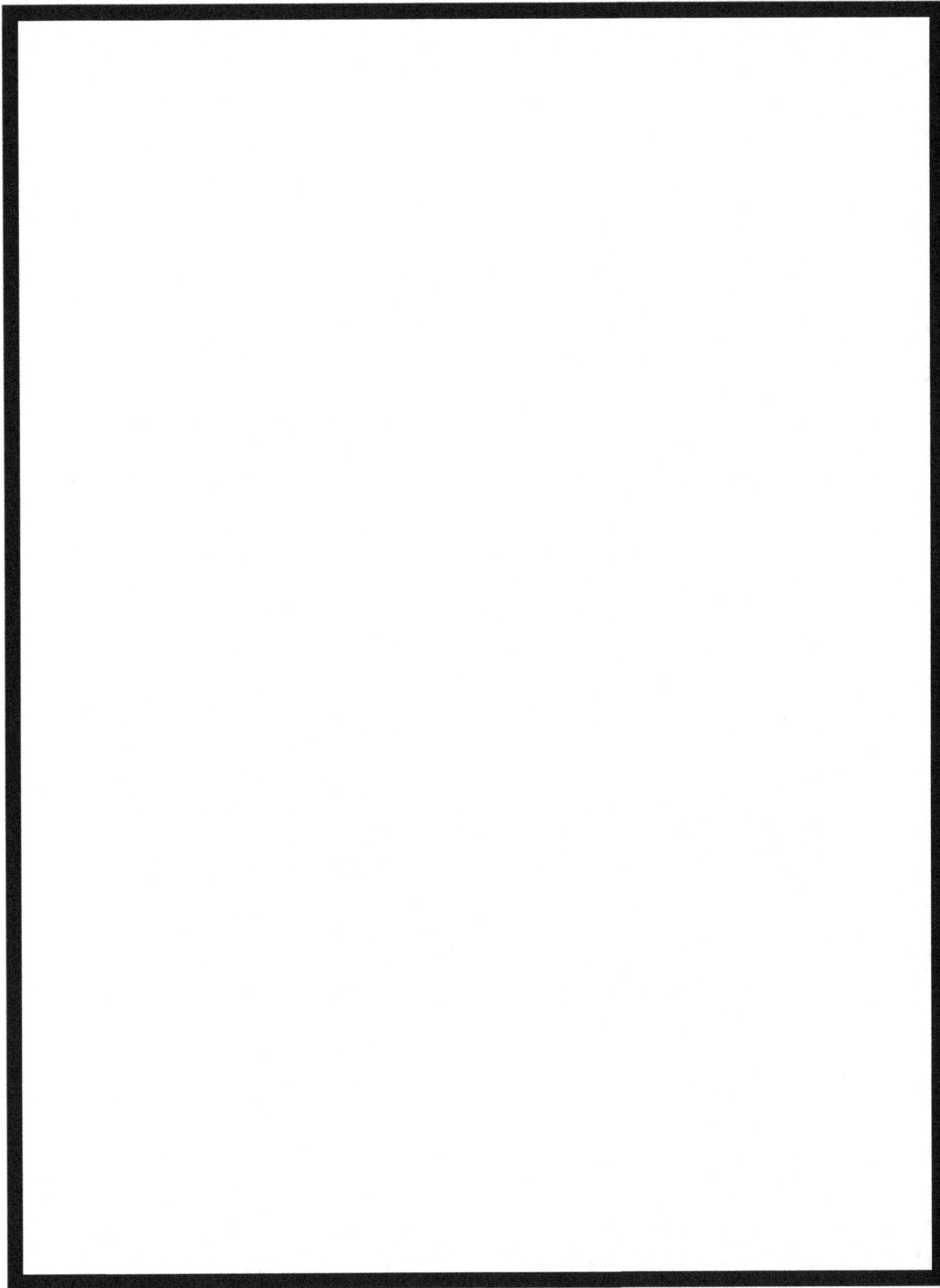

HE DIED DOING WHAT HE LOVED, ANNOYING THE HELL OUT OF ME AND NOT BELIEVING THAT I WOULD STAB HIM.

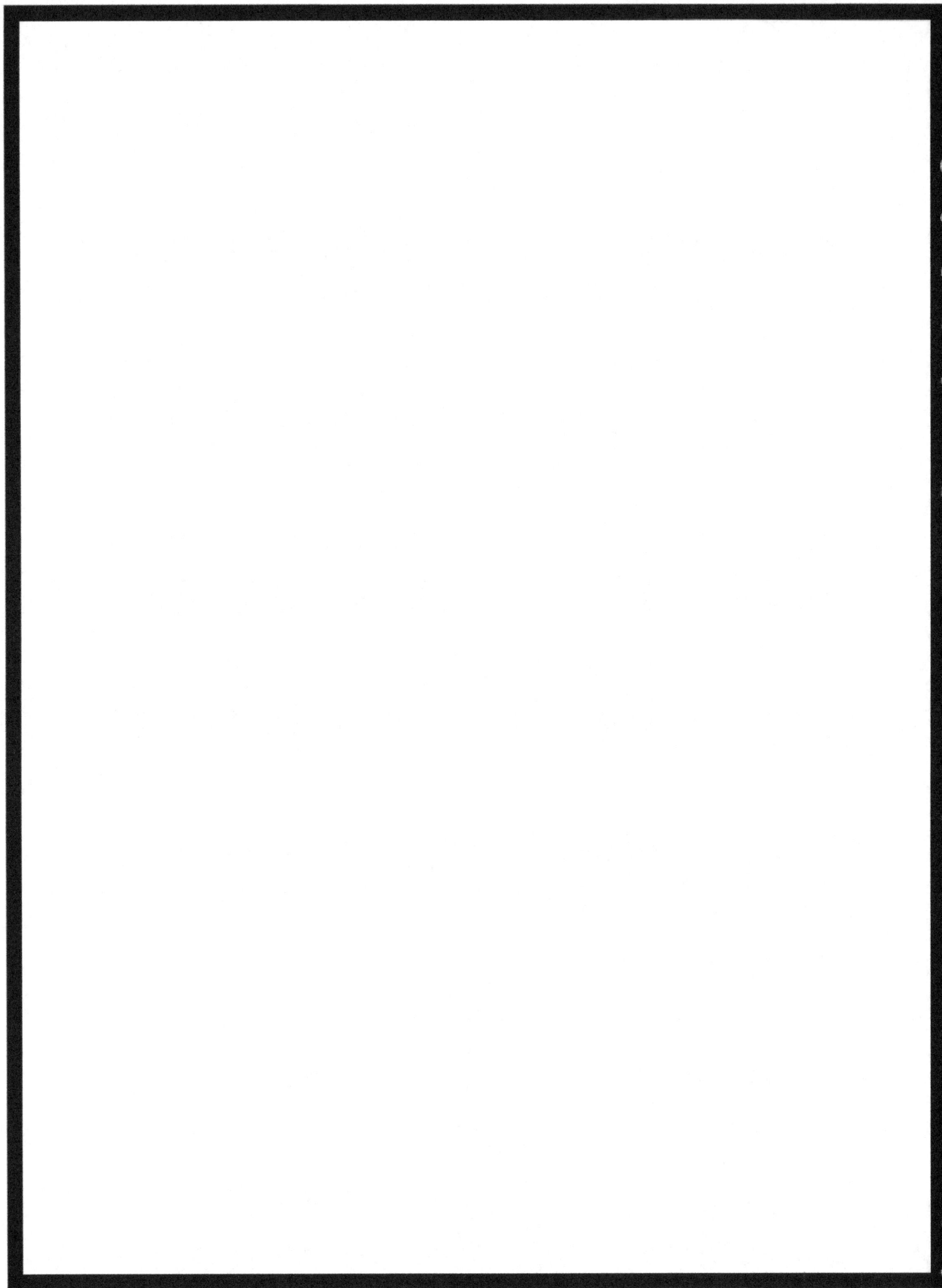

THIS KILLING THEM WITH KINDNESS IS TAKING WAY LONGER THAN EXPECTED...

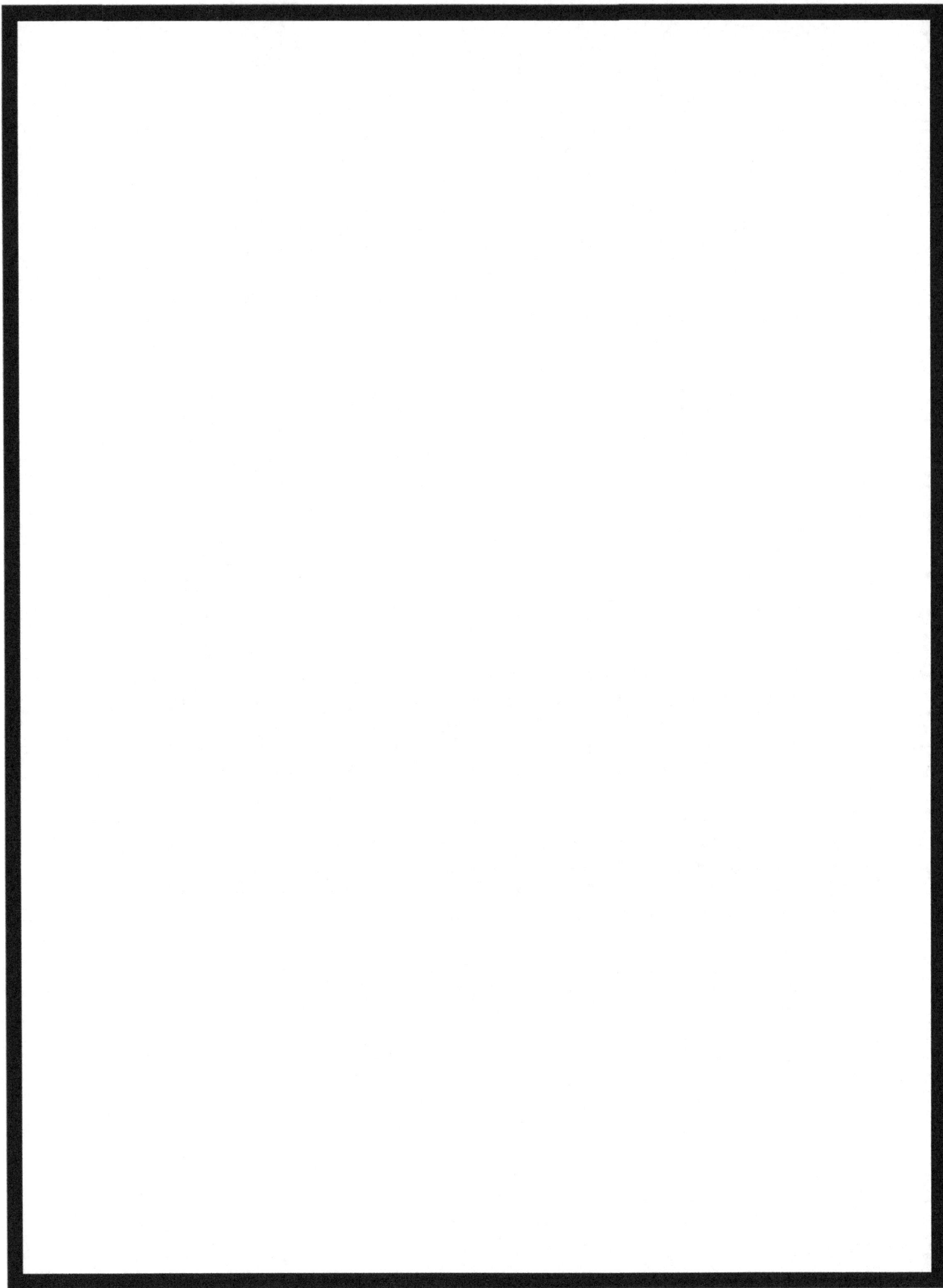

Hmmm, I'm going to "file your opinions" right here between "fuck this" and "fuck that"

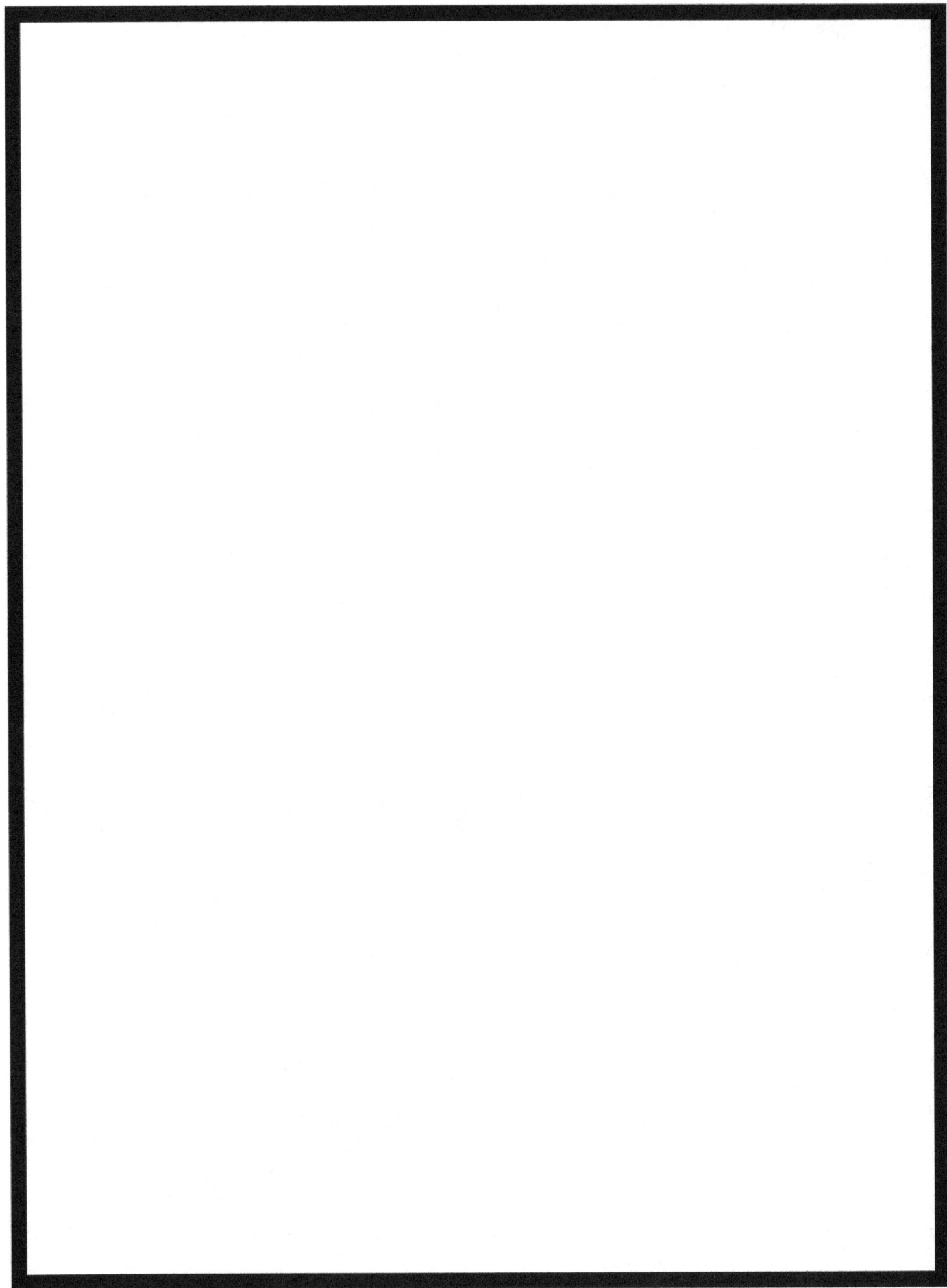

Saw a piece of shit on the ground today, it reminded me of you

I JUST CHECKED MY BALANCE AT THE ATM. IT PRINTED ME COUPONS.

THROW LAMPS AT
PEOPLE WHO
NEED TO
LIGHTEN
THE
fuck up

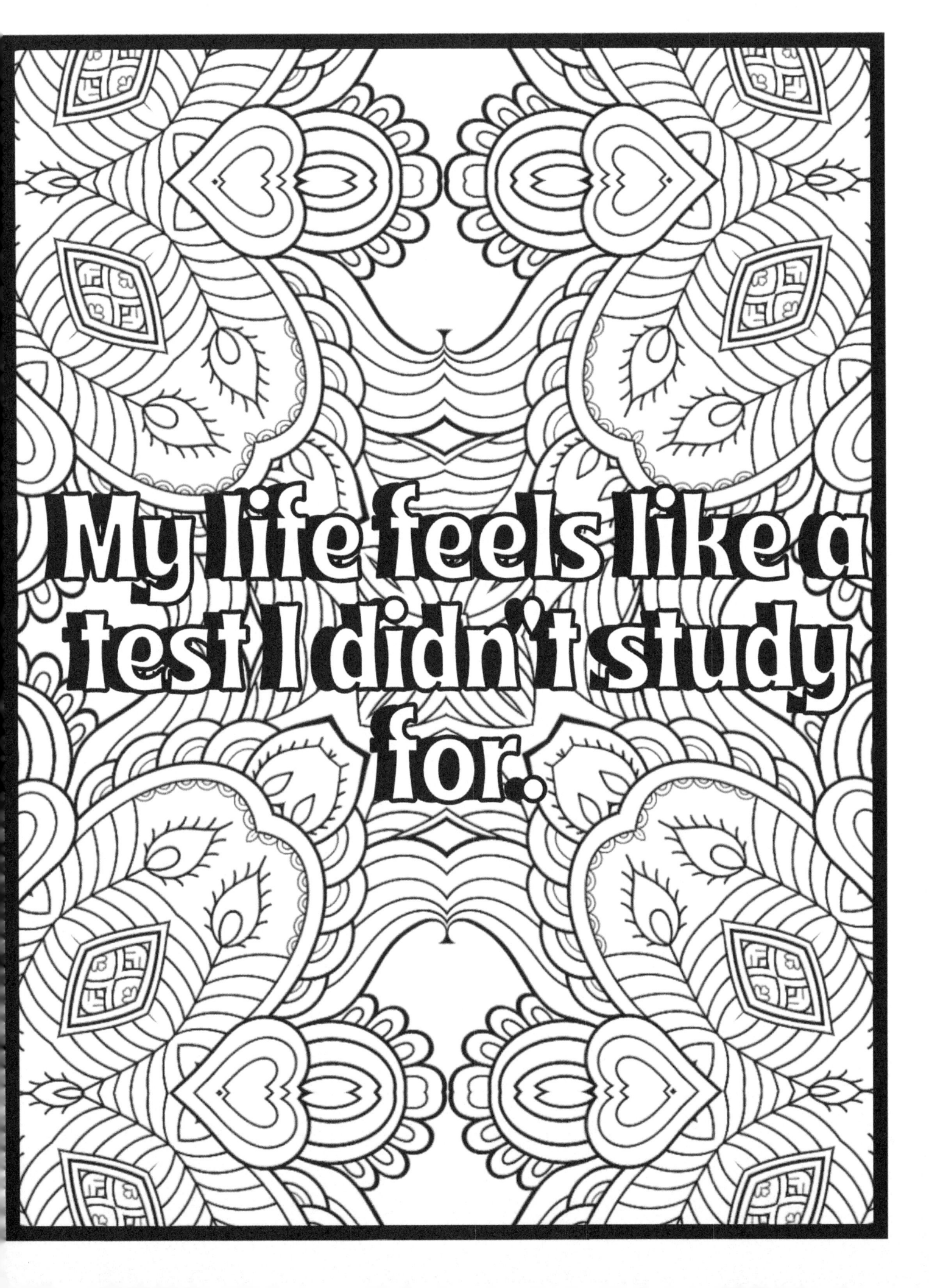

My life feels like a test I didn't study for.

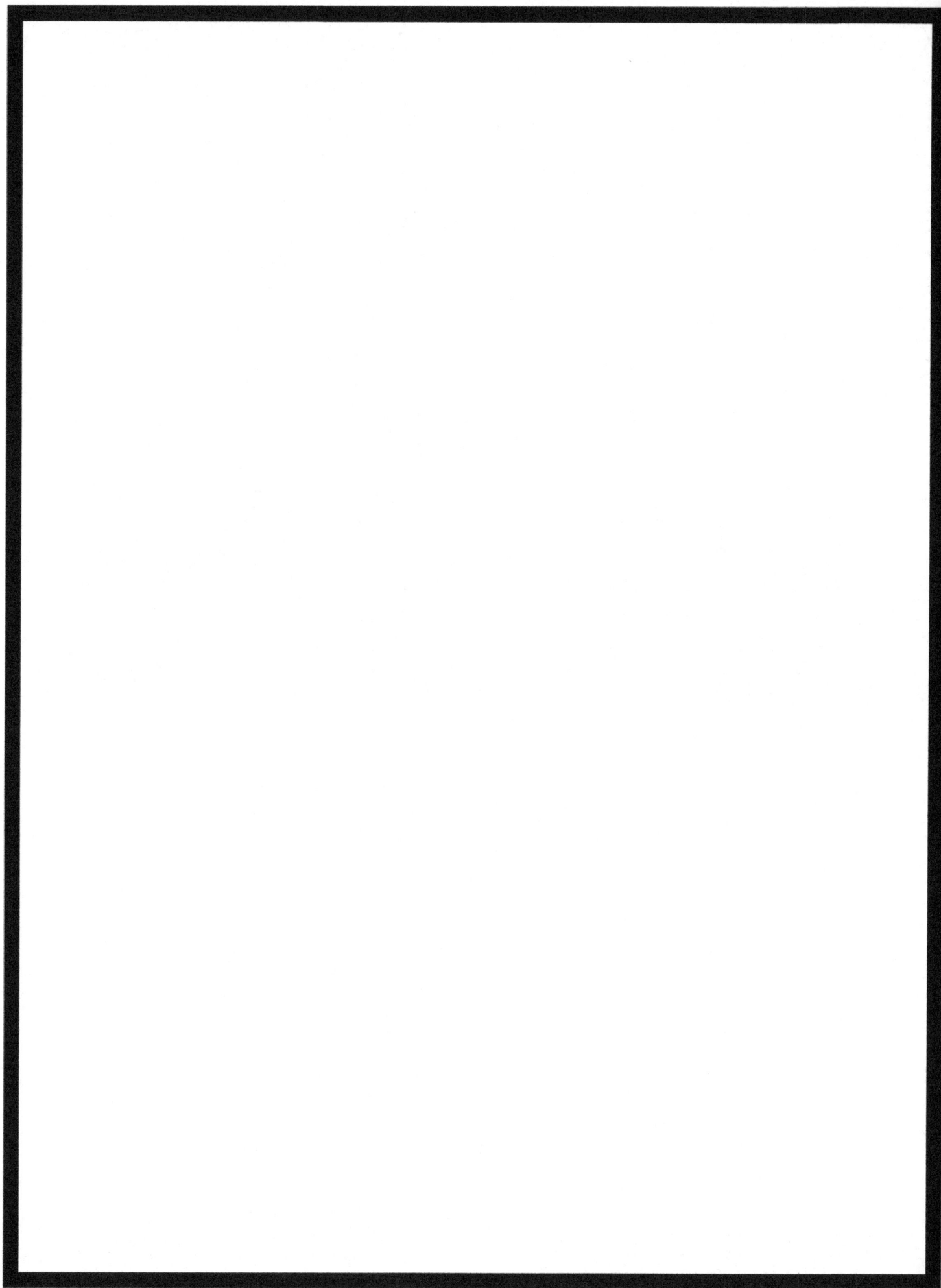

YOU SHOULD EAT SOME MAKEUP SO YOU CAN BE PRETTY ON THE INSIDE TOO

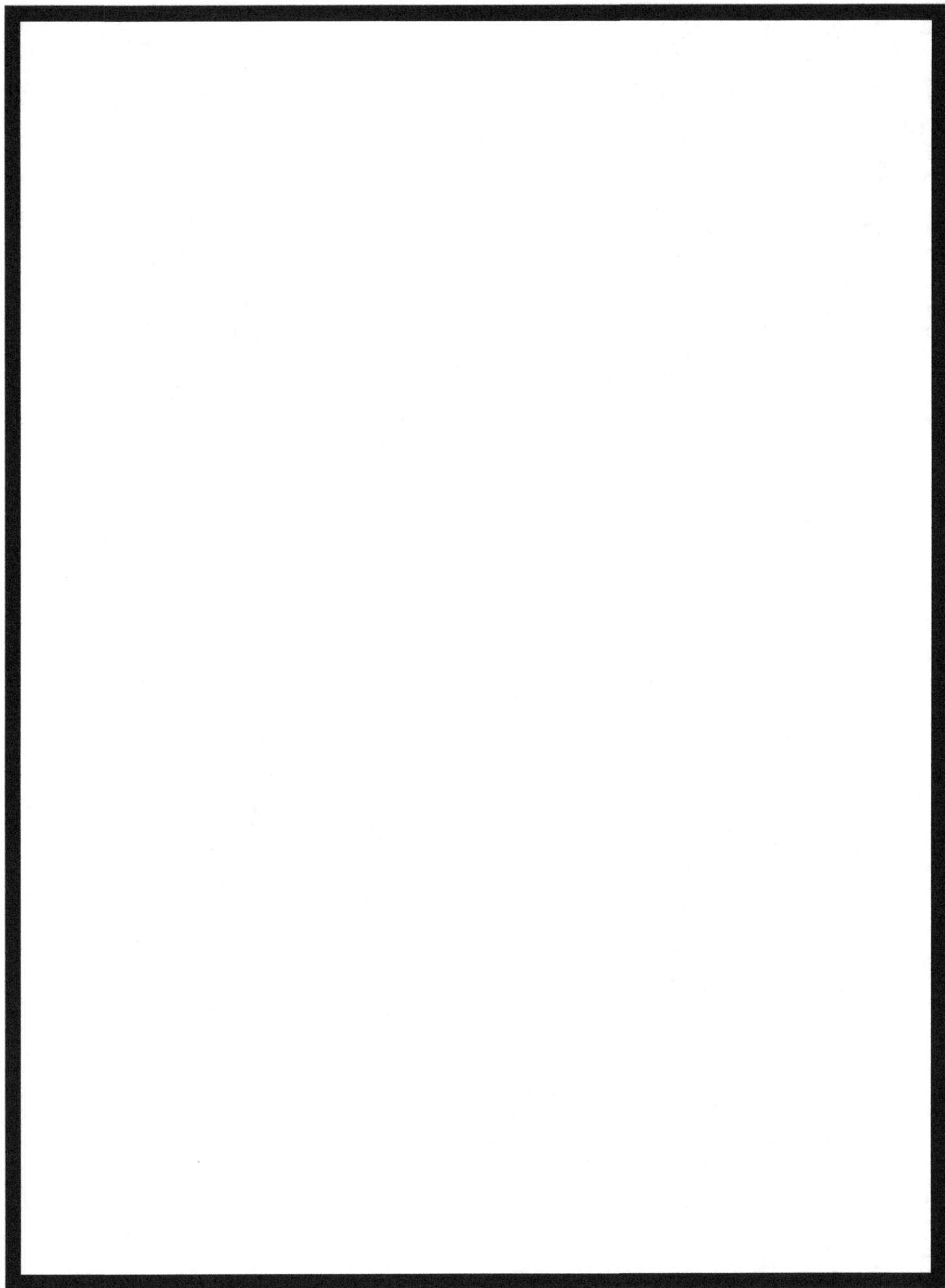

If you ran like your mouth, you'd be in good shape

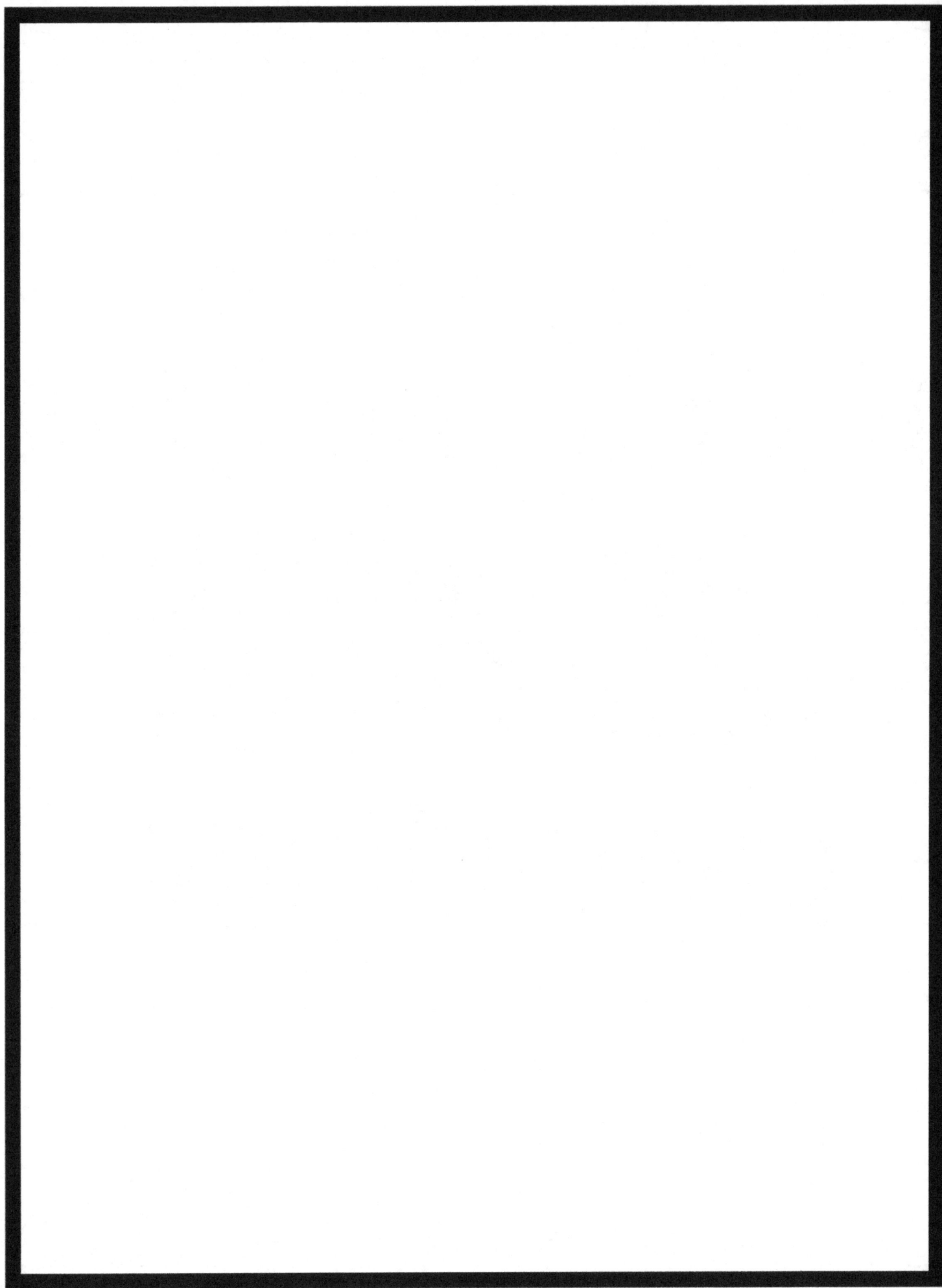

IF YOU WALK A MILE IN MY SHOES, YOU'LL END UP IN A BAR DRINKING A BEER

I've got heels higher than your standards.

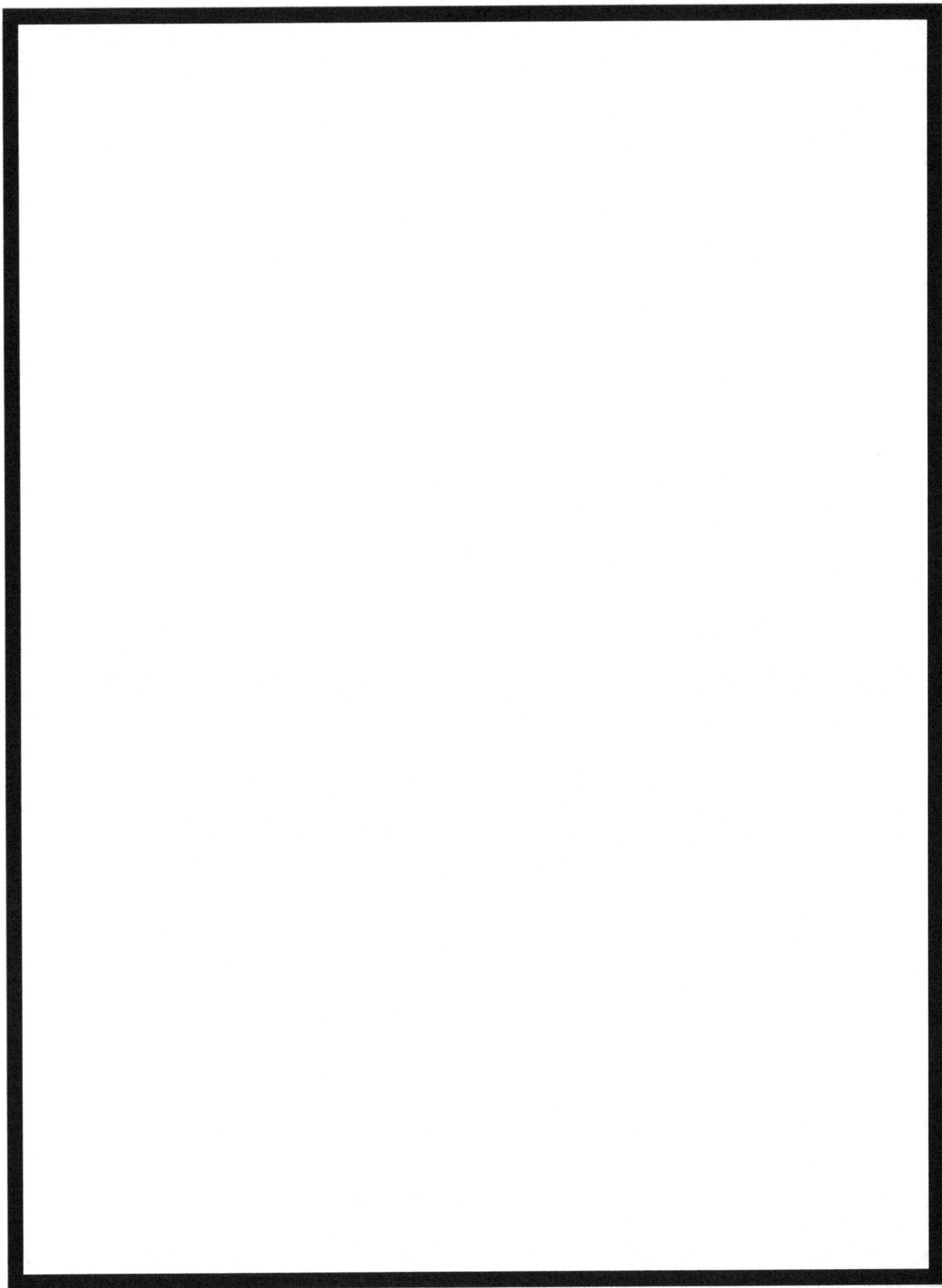

THEY ALWAYS SAY THERE'S A PERSON CAPABLE OF MURDER IN EVERY FRIENDSHIP GROUP.

I SUSPECTED IT WAS DAVE, SO I KILLED HIM BEFORE HE COULD CAUSE ANY HARM

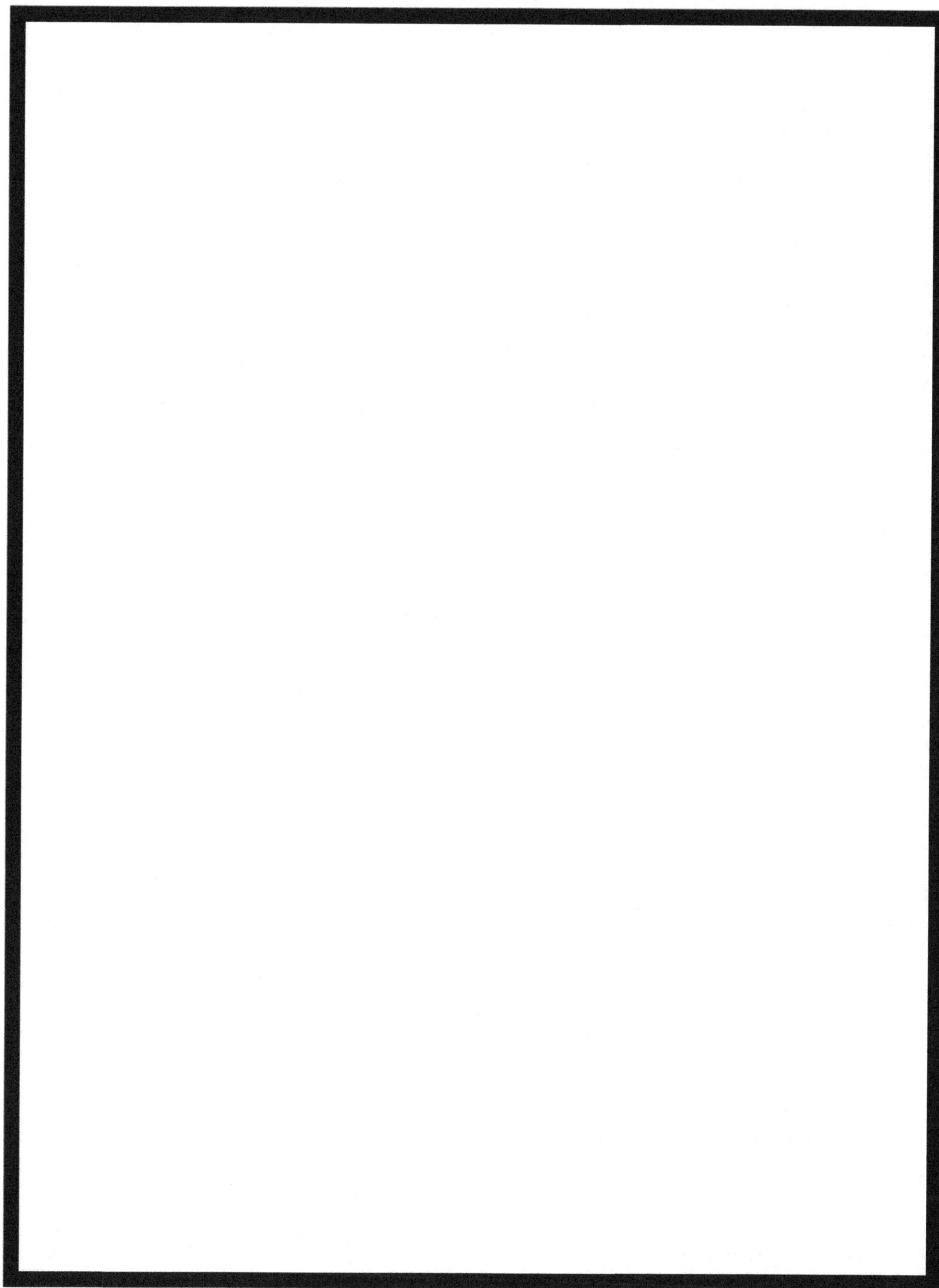

"It's not about how tired you are, it's about how tired you're making everyone else"
-My husband explaining bedtime to the kids

-ME DEALING WITH LIFE

"....I'm gonna order a pizza."

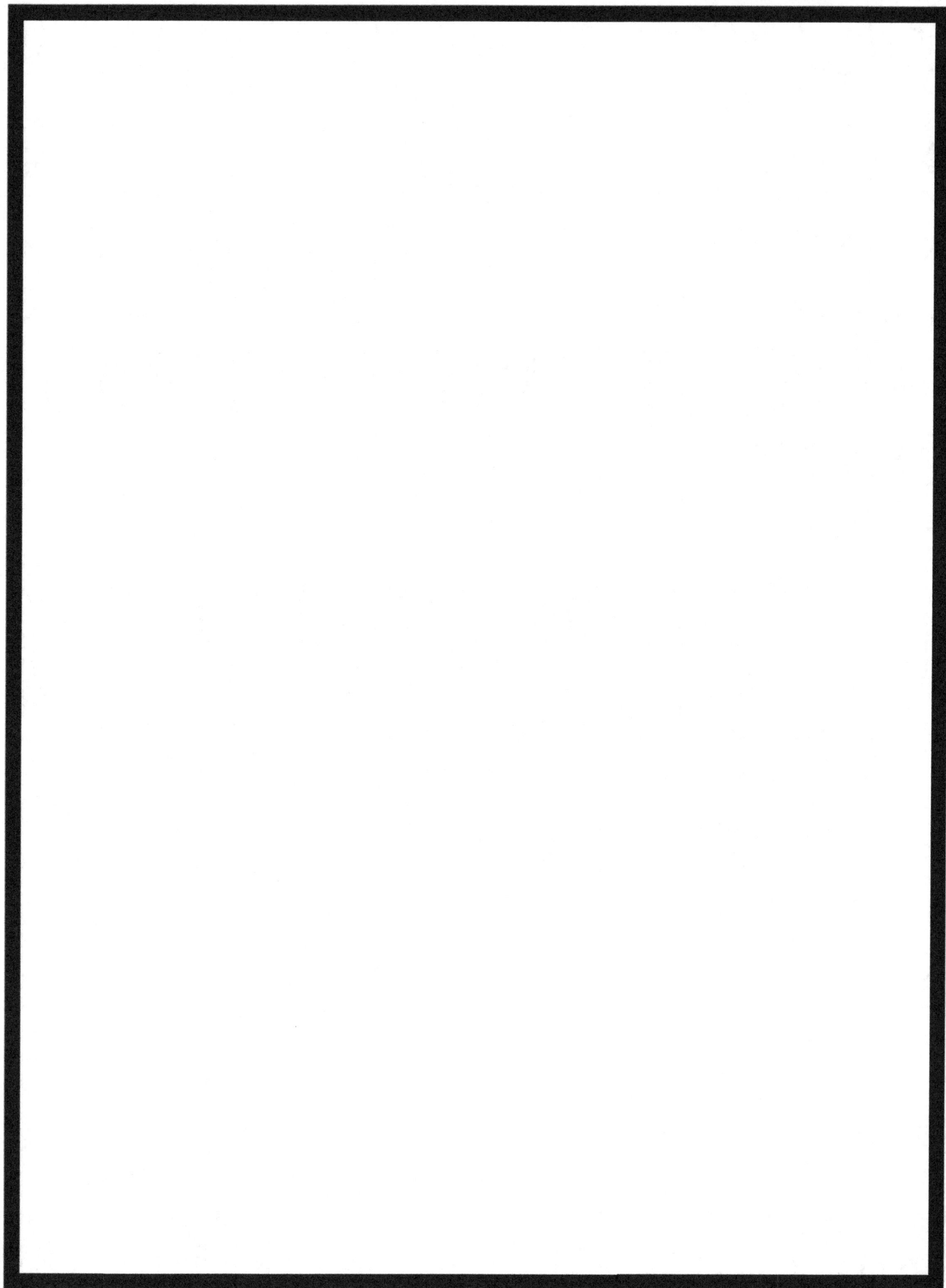

I ASKED MY HUSBAND AM I THE ONLY ONE YOU'VE BEEN WITH. HE SAID YES, THE OTHERS WERE ALL NINES AND TENS

SEND BAIL MONEY

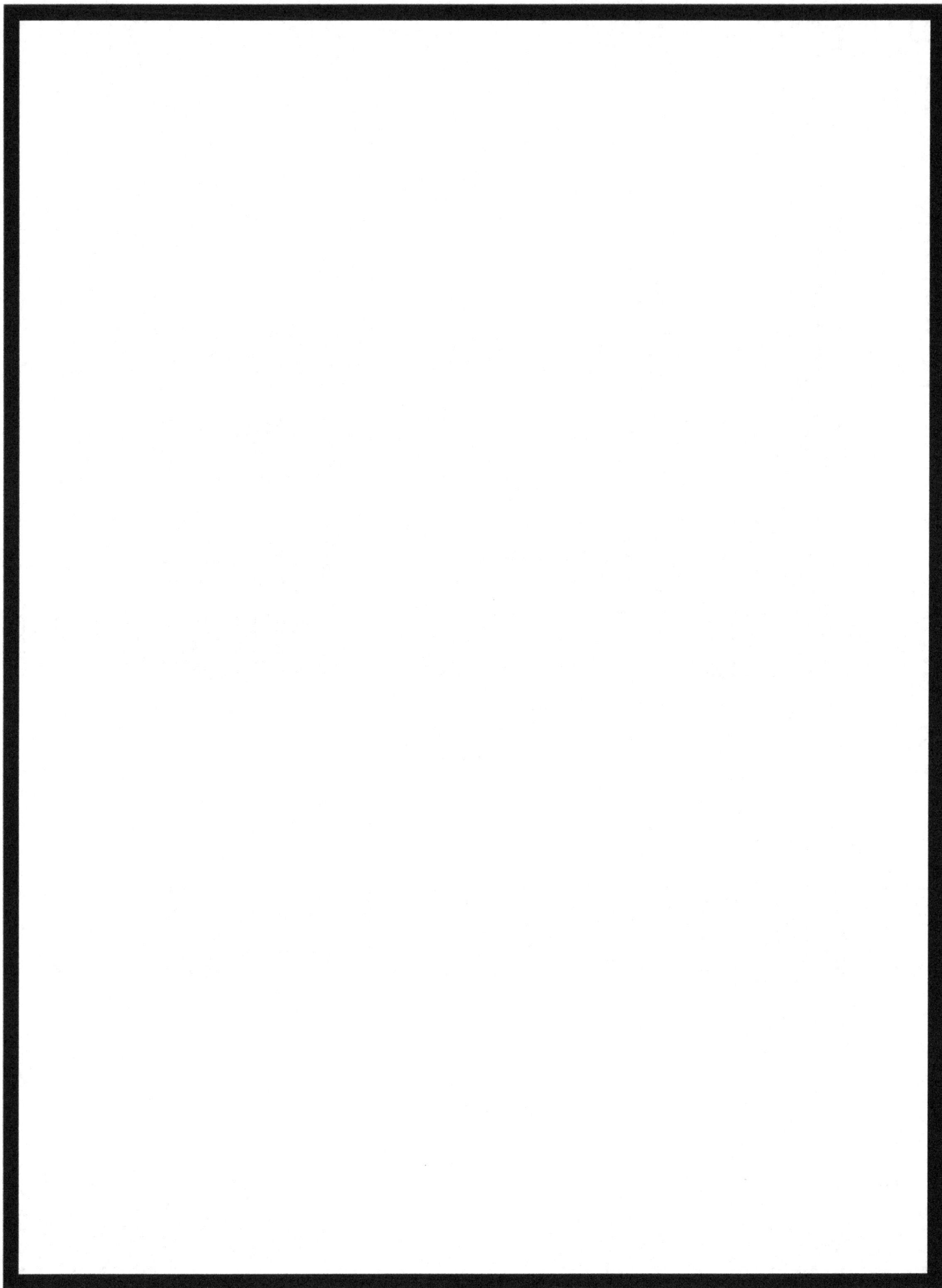

MY HUSBAND IS MAD I HAVE NO SENSE OF DIRECTION. SO I PACKED MY STUFF AND *RIGHT*

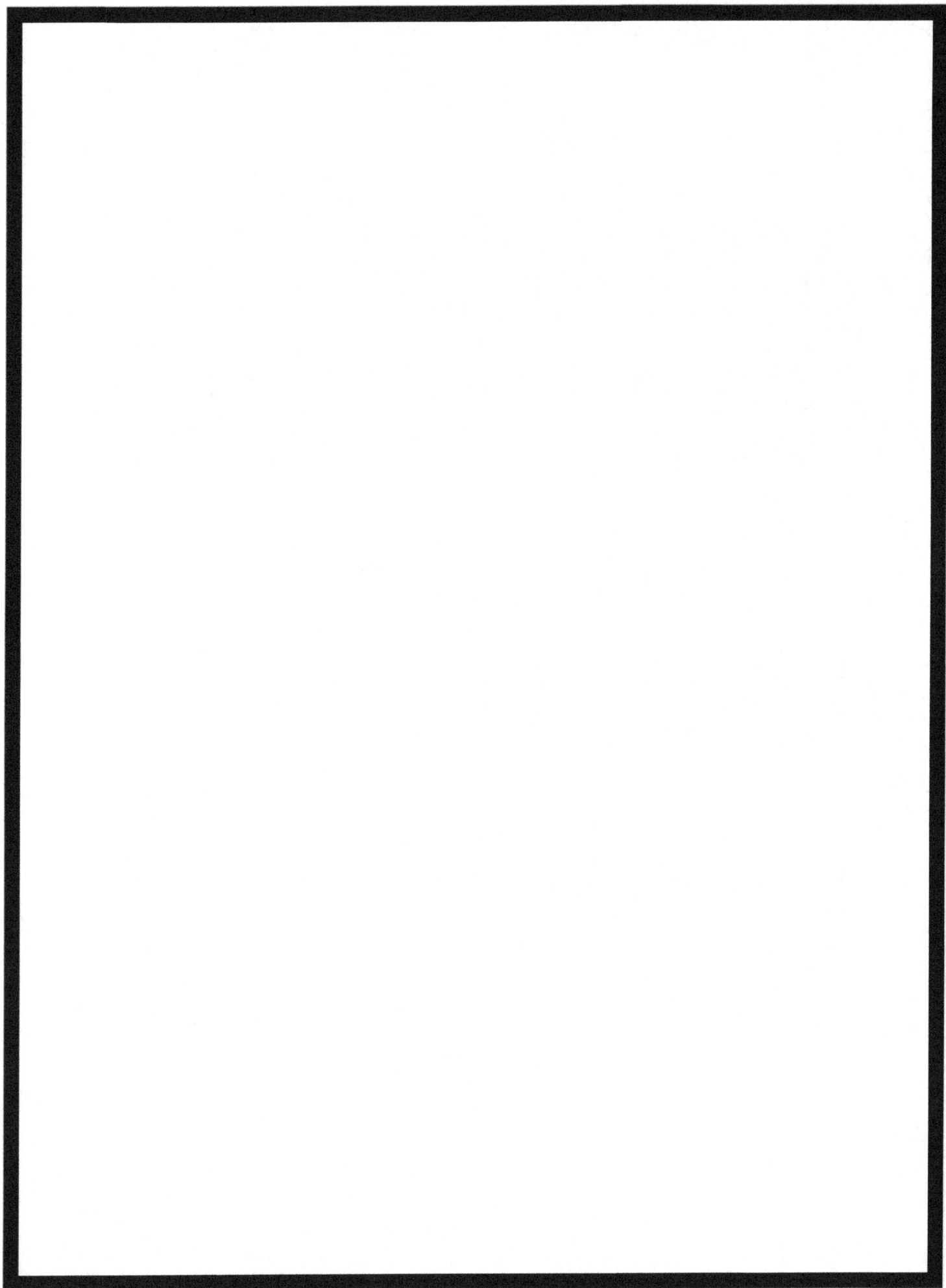

YOU KNOW YOU'RE NOT LIKED WHEN THEY HAND YOU THE CAMERA EVERY TIME THEY MAKE A GROUP PHOTO

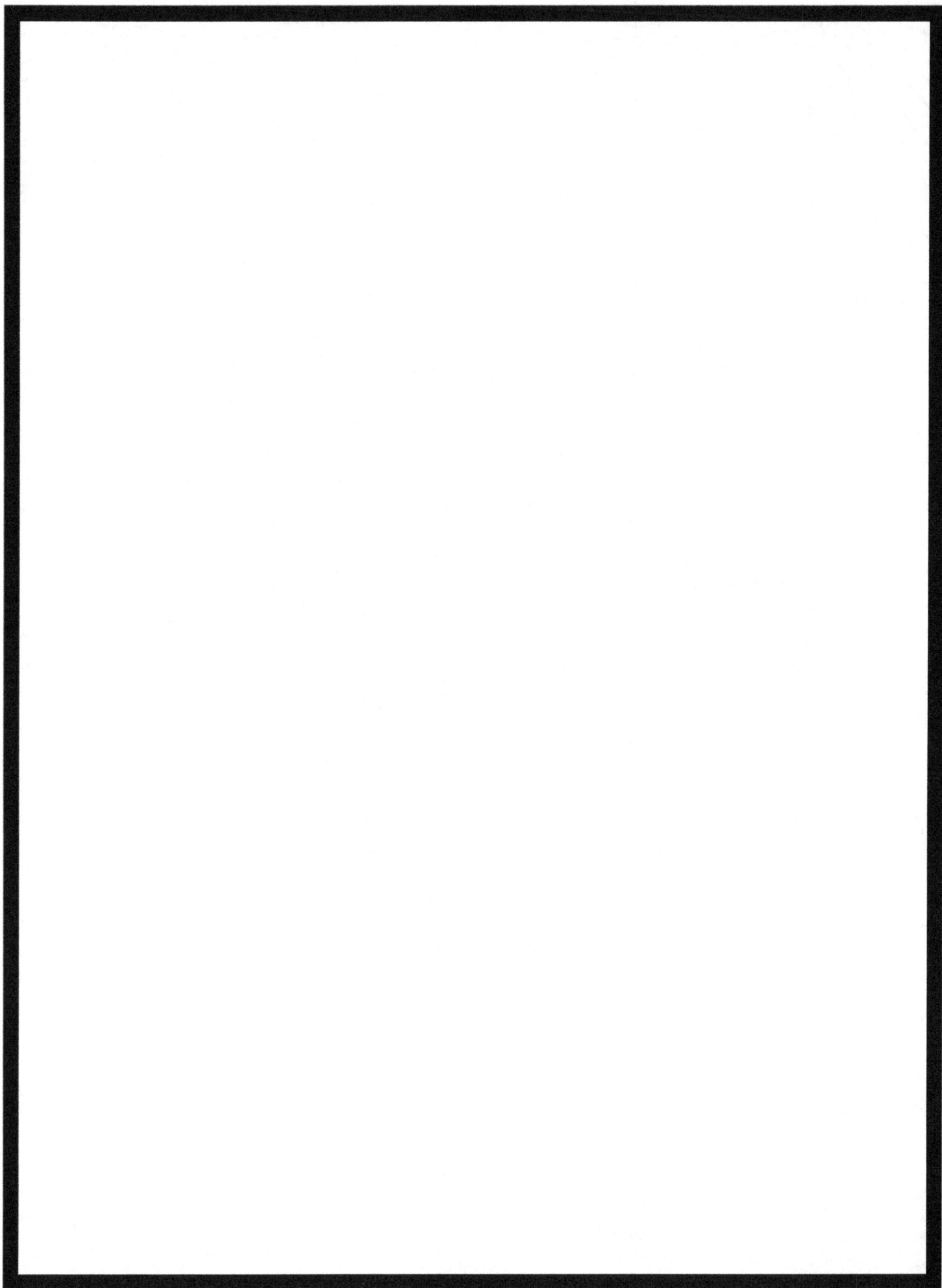

You're not completely useless... You can always serve as a bad example

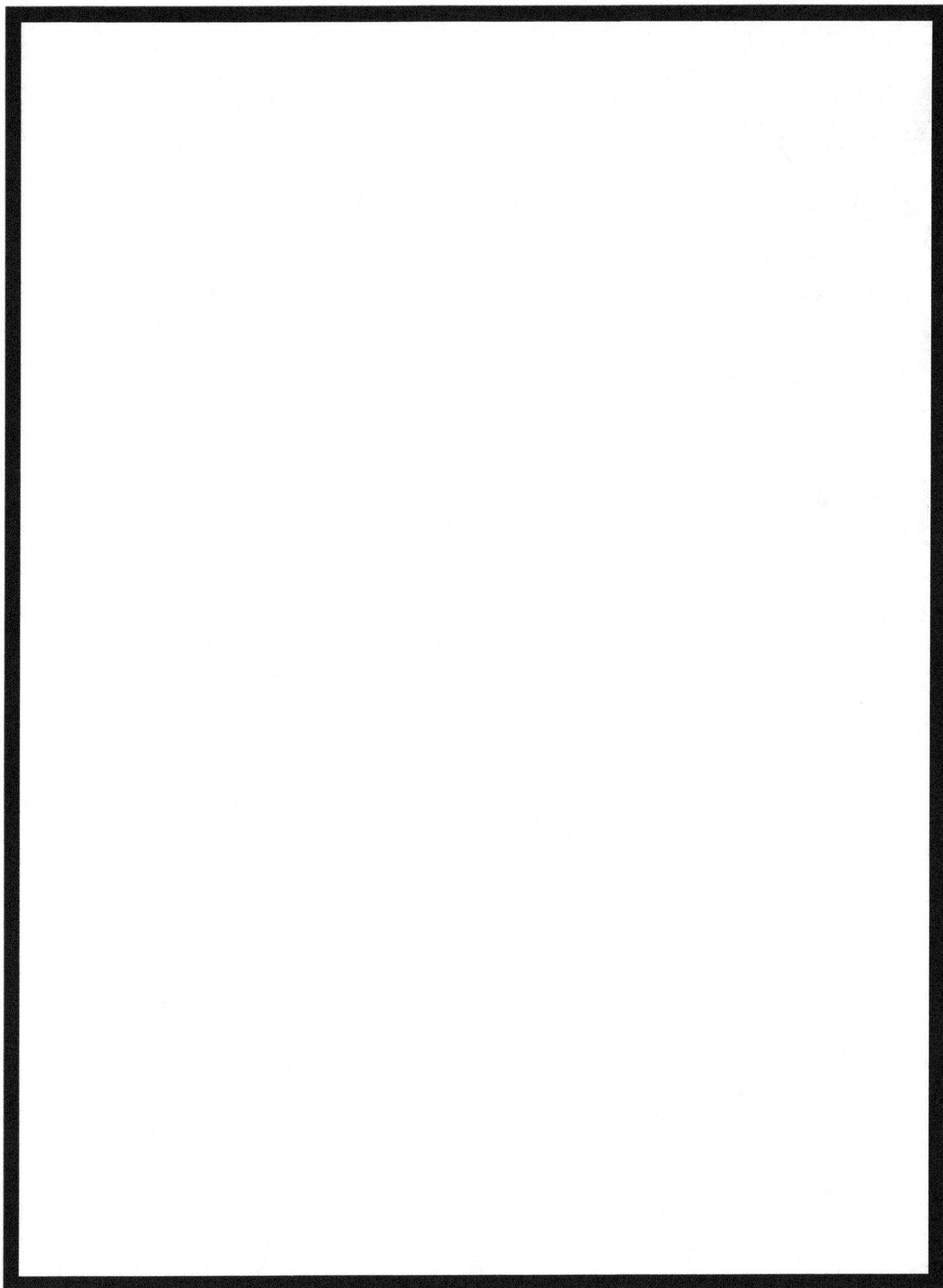

My boss told me to have a good day. So I went home.

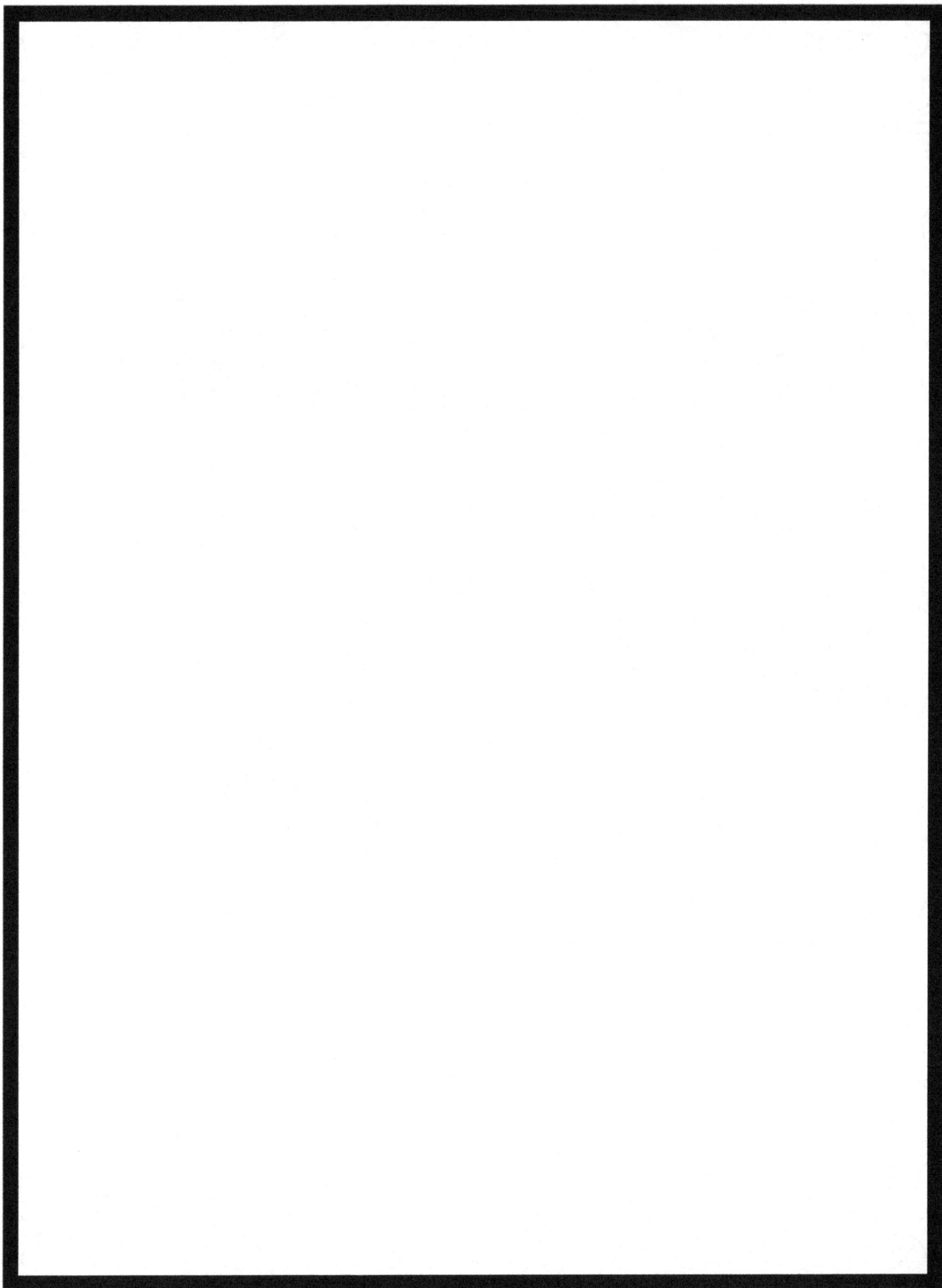

IT'S BEEN A ROUGH WEEK. BUT I DIDN'T NEED BAIL MONEY, SO IT COULD HAVE BEEN WORSE

Me? Overreacting? Shit probably

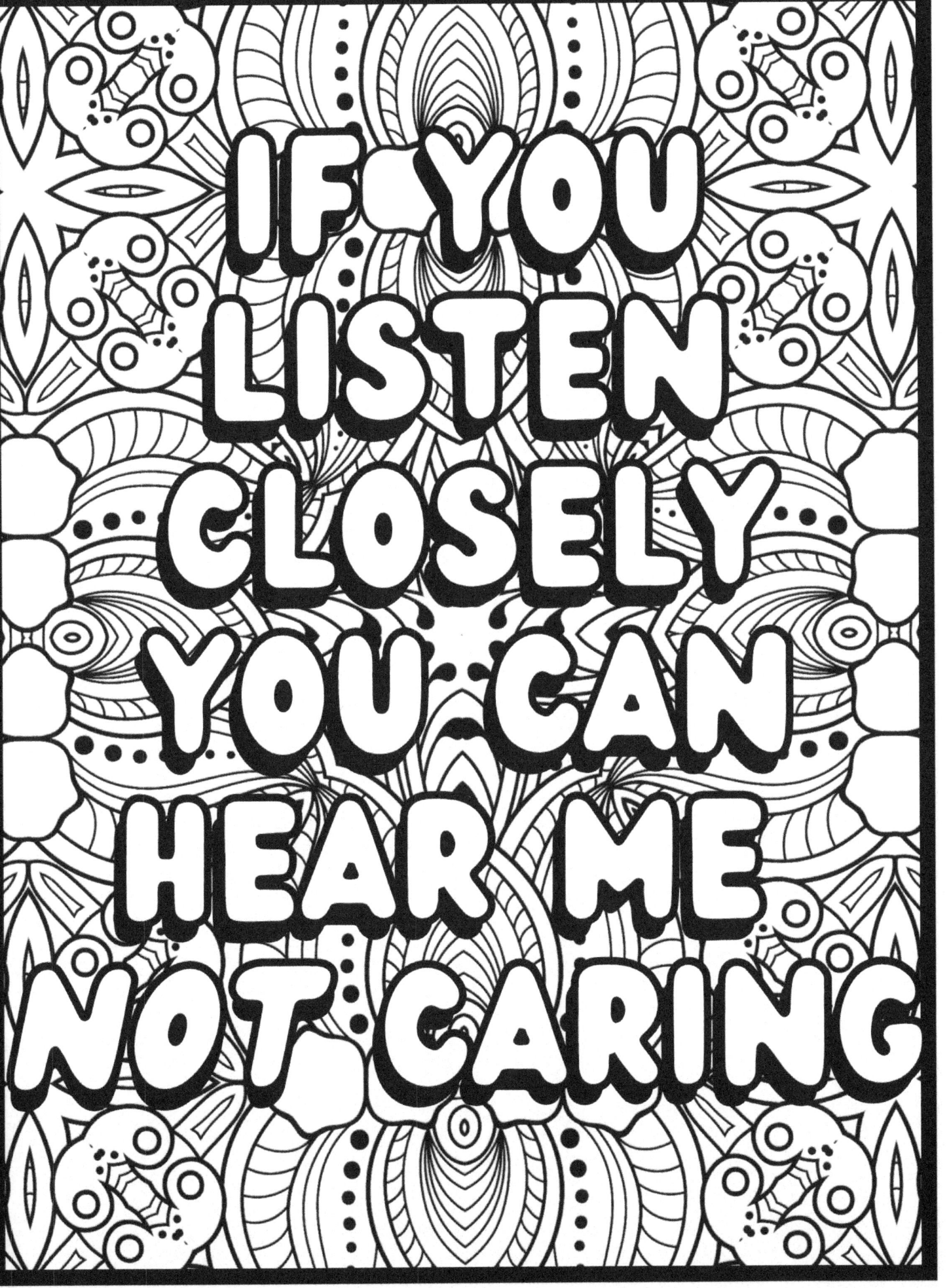

IF YOU LISTEN CLOSELY YOU CAN HEAR ME NOT CARING

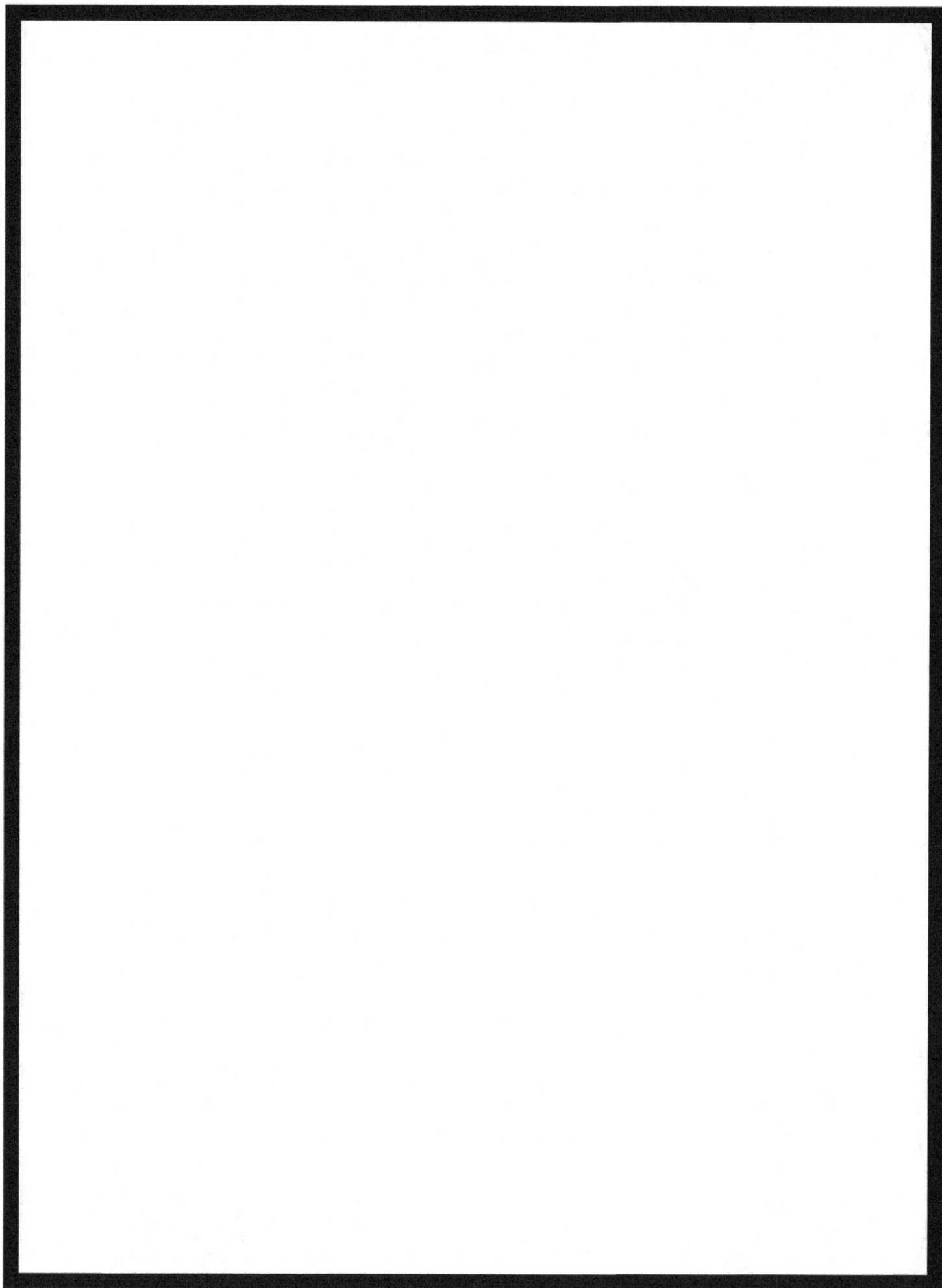

...on the BRIGHT side I'm NOT addicted TO COCAINE

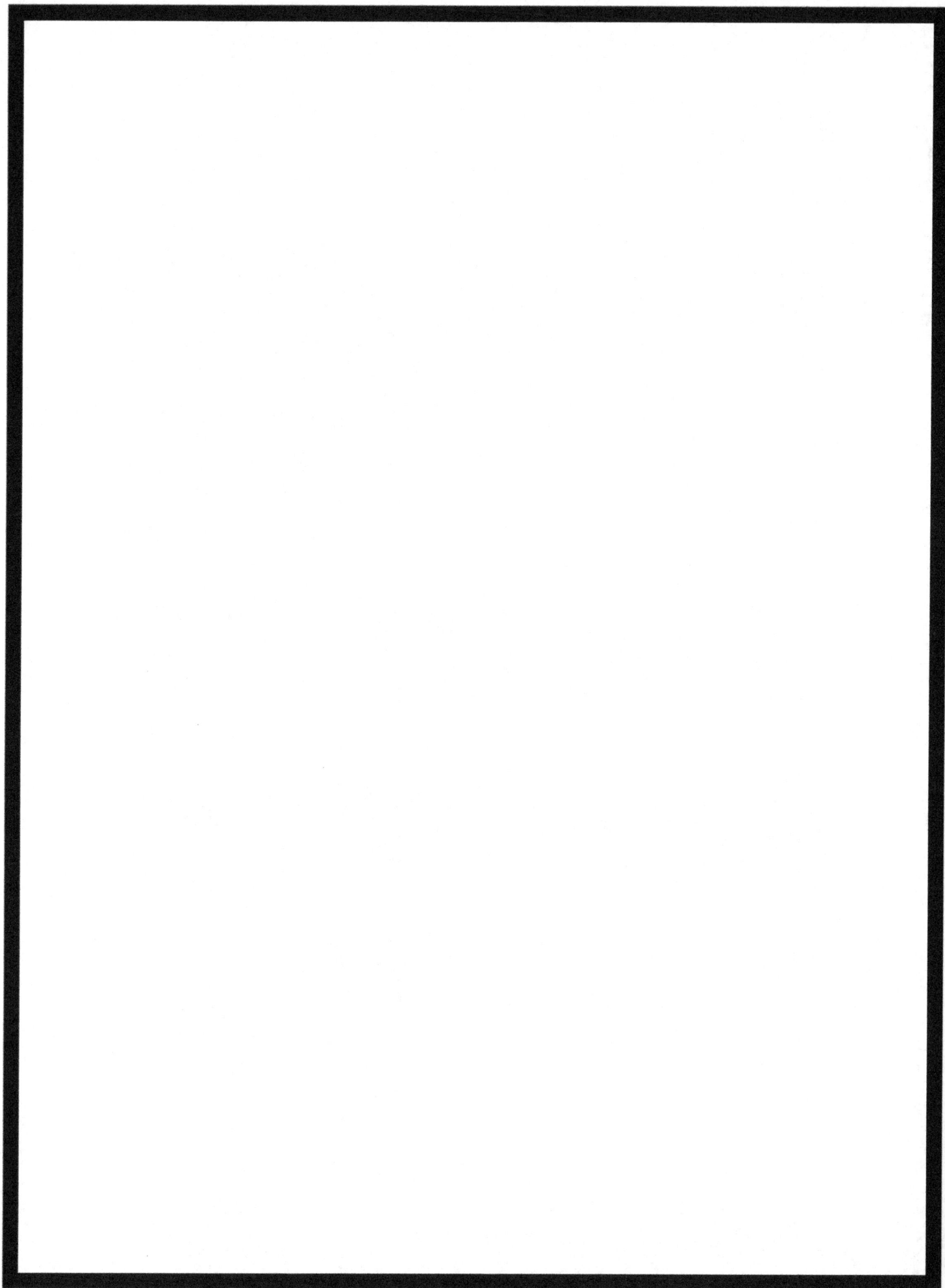

Coffee

MAKES ME FEEL

LESS

MURDERY

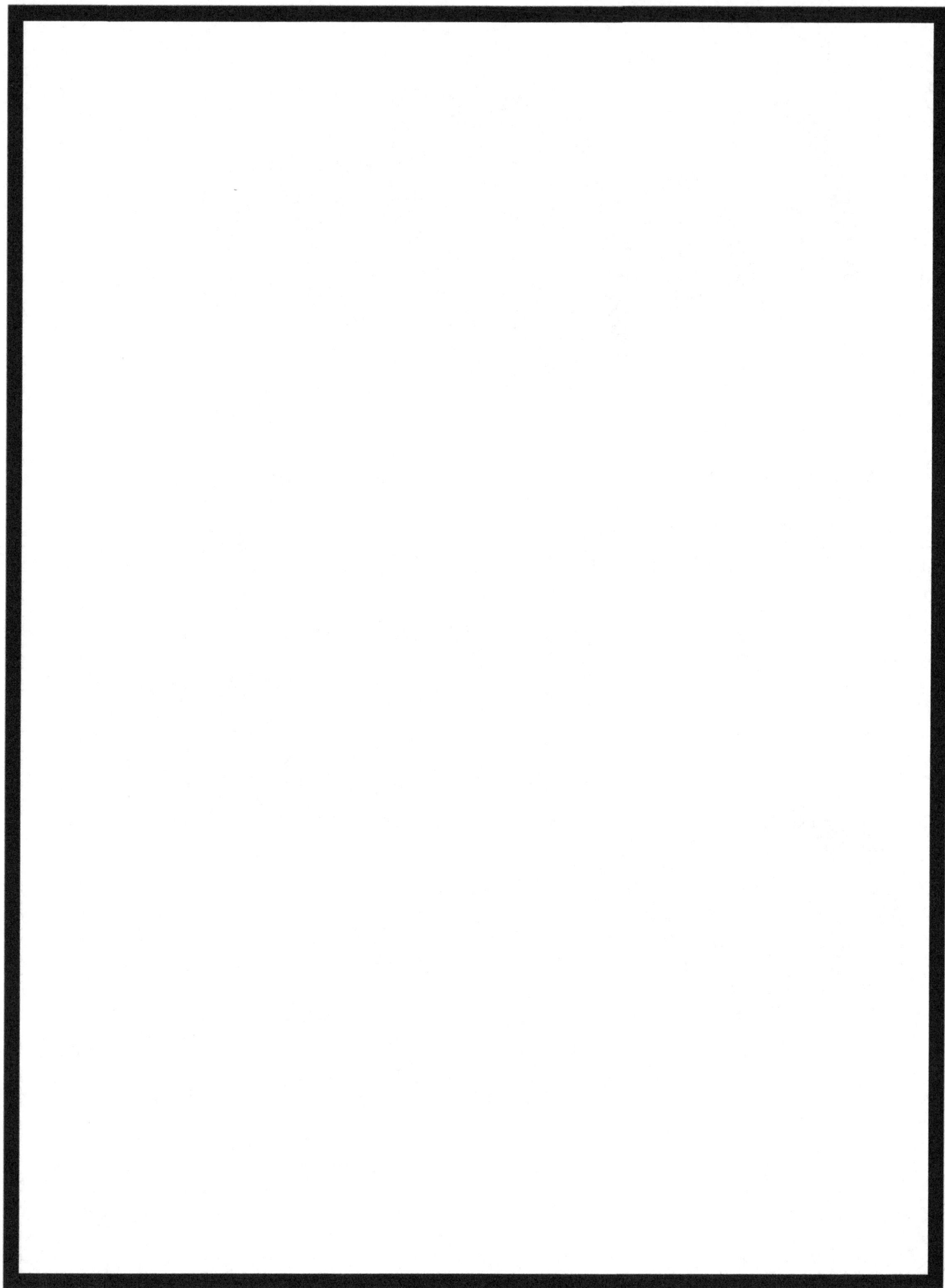

WHAT doesn't KILL you GIVES YOU ALOT OF UNHEALTHY COPING MECHANISMS and a really dark sense of HUMOR

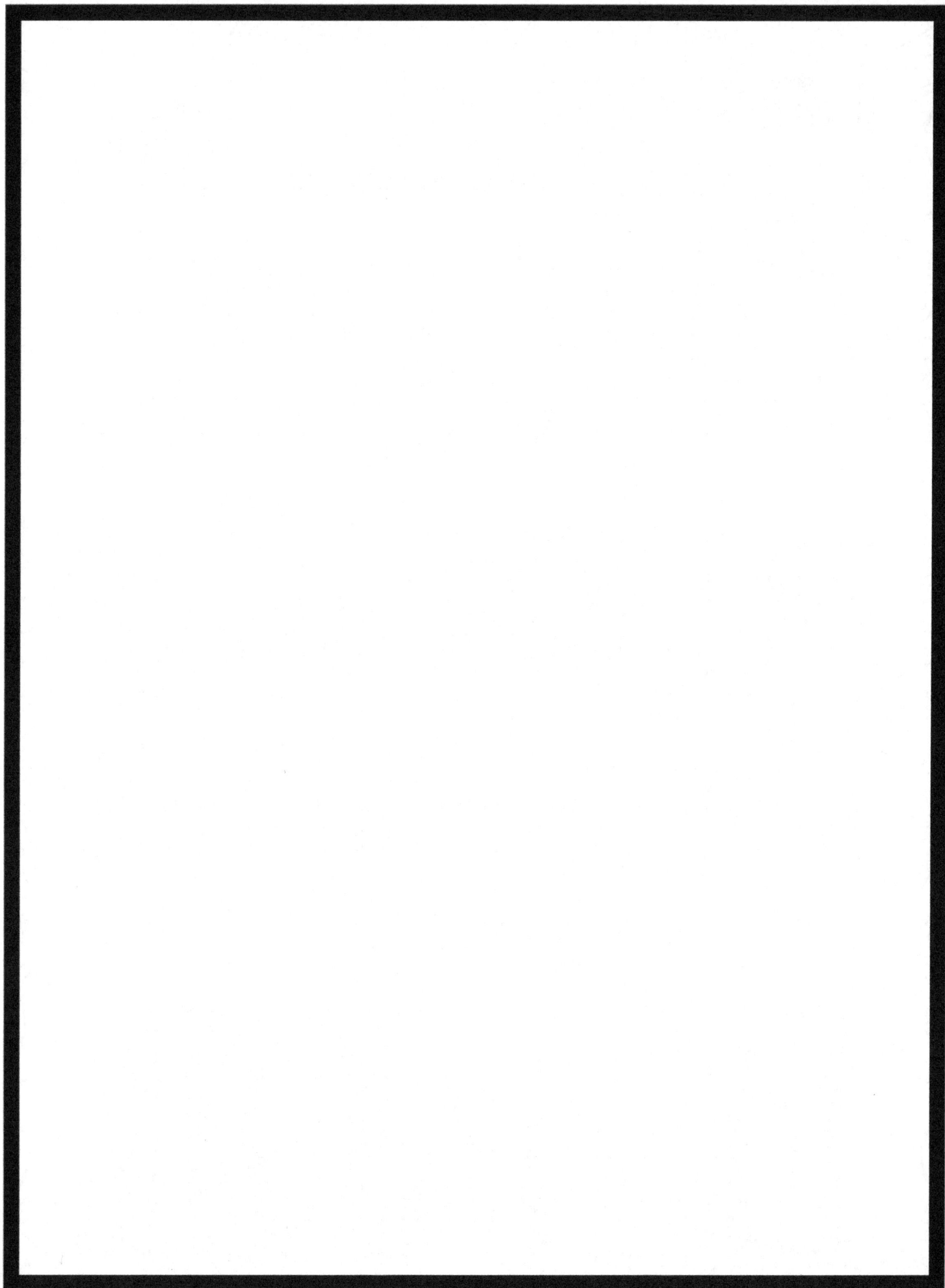

Just tell me *when* and *where* and I'll be there **20 minutes** *late*

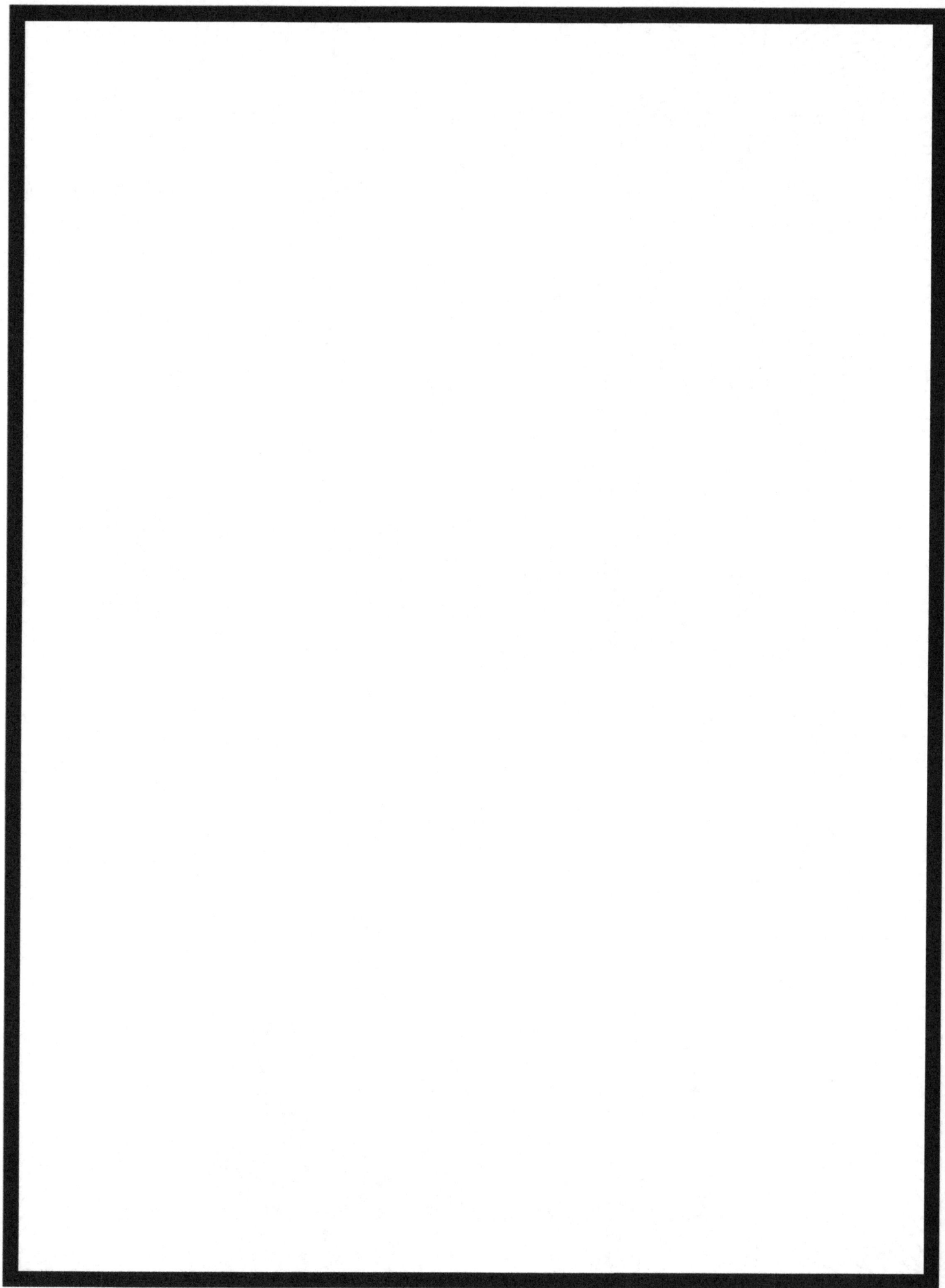

HARD WORK NEVER KILLED ANYONE, BUT WHY TAKE A CHANCE

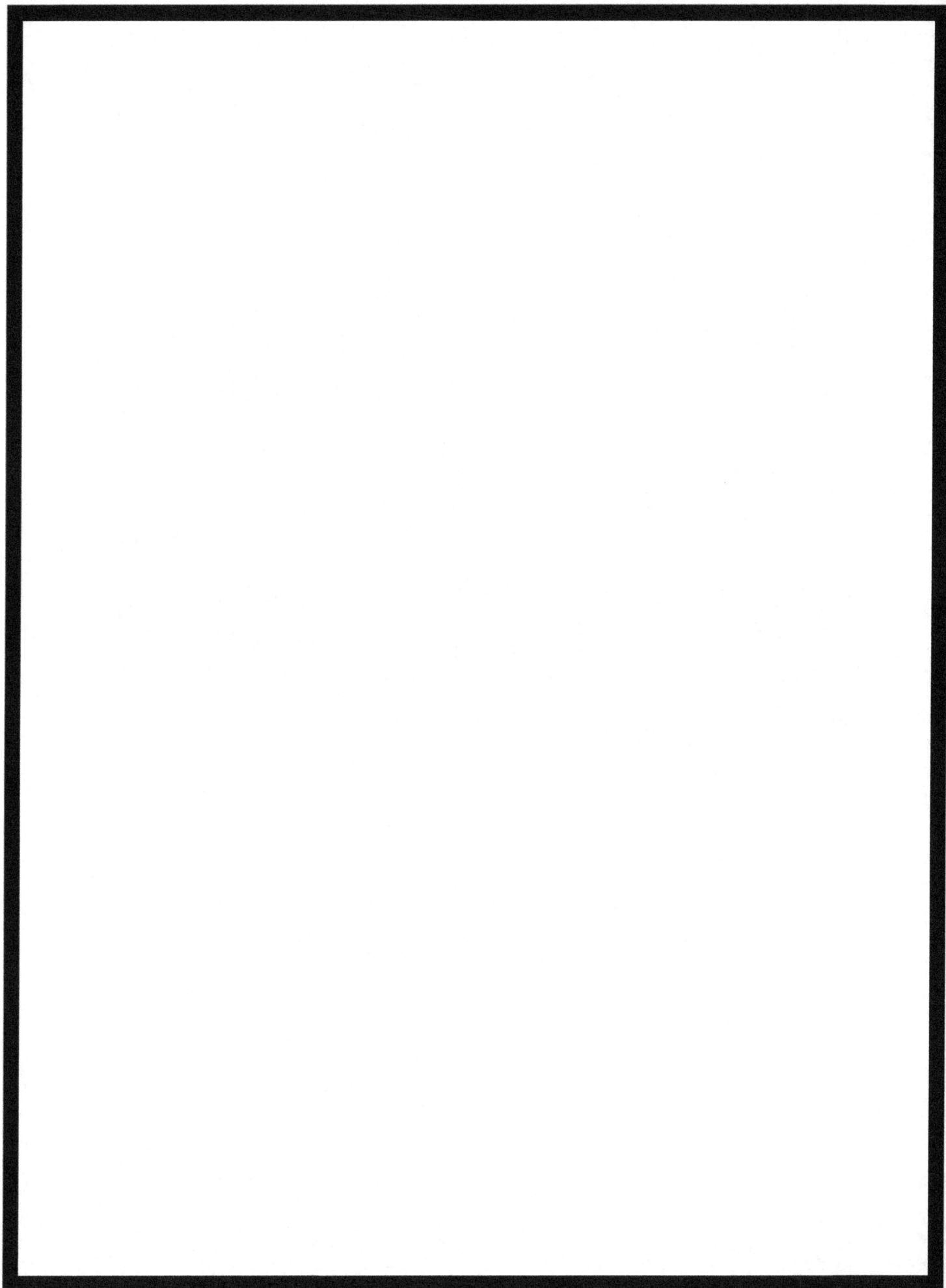

Dear life... CAN YOU AT LEAST START USING lubricant

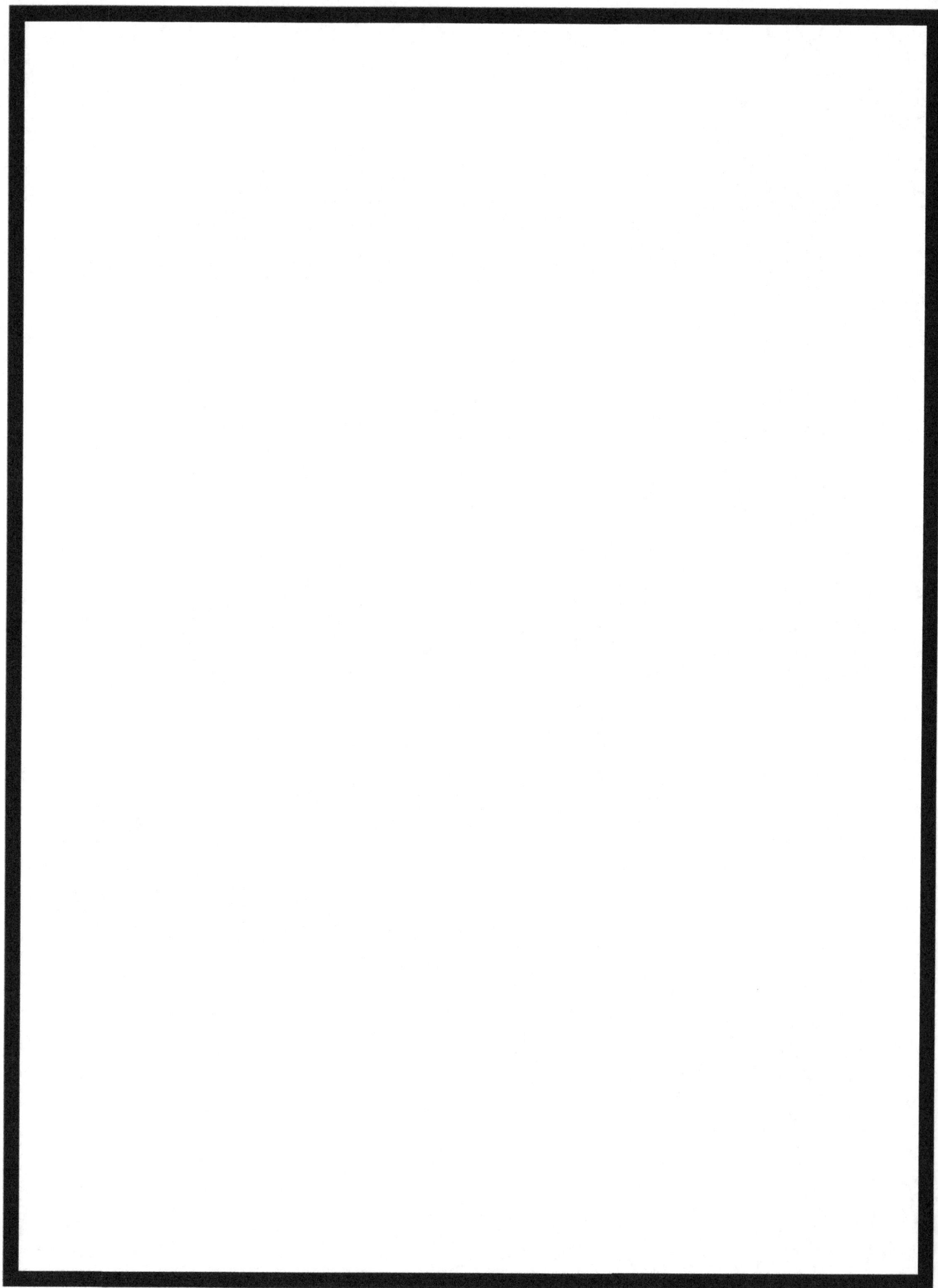

OH YOU'RE OFFENDED... I'M SURE I HAVE SOME THICKER SKIN FOR YOU IN THE BACK.

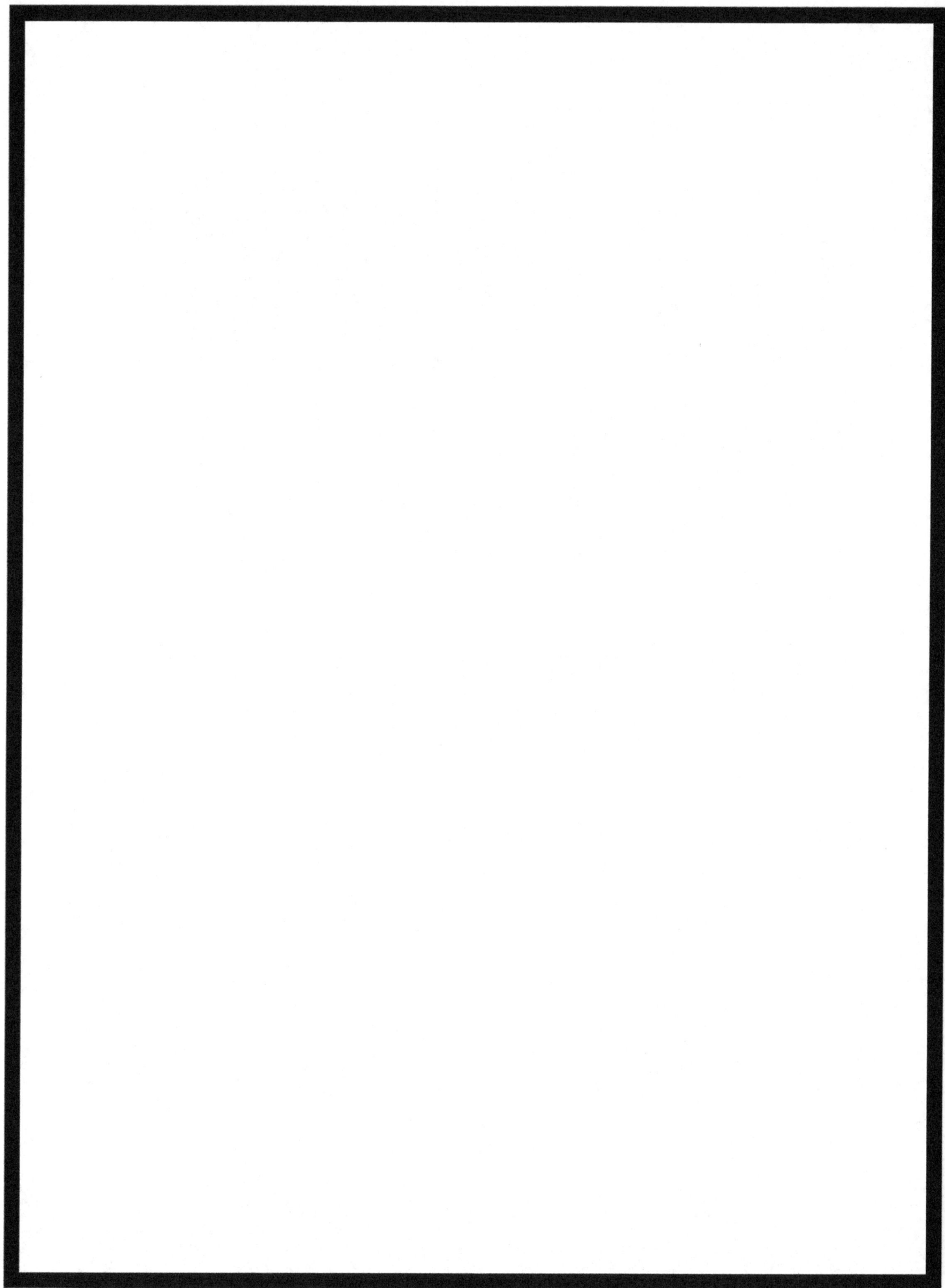

Four out of five voices in my head are telling me your an idiot. The other one is deciding where to BURY you.

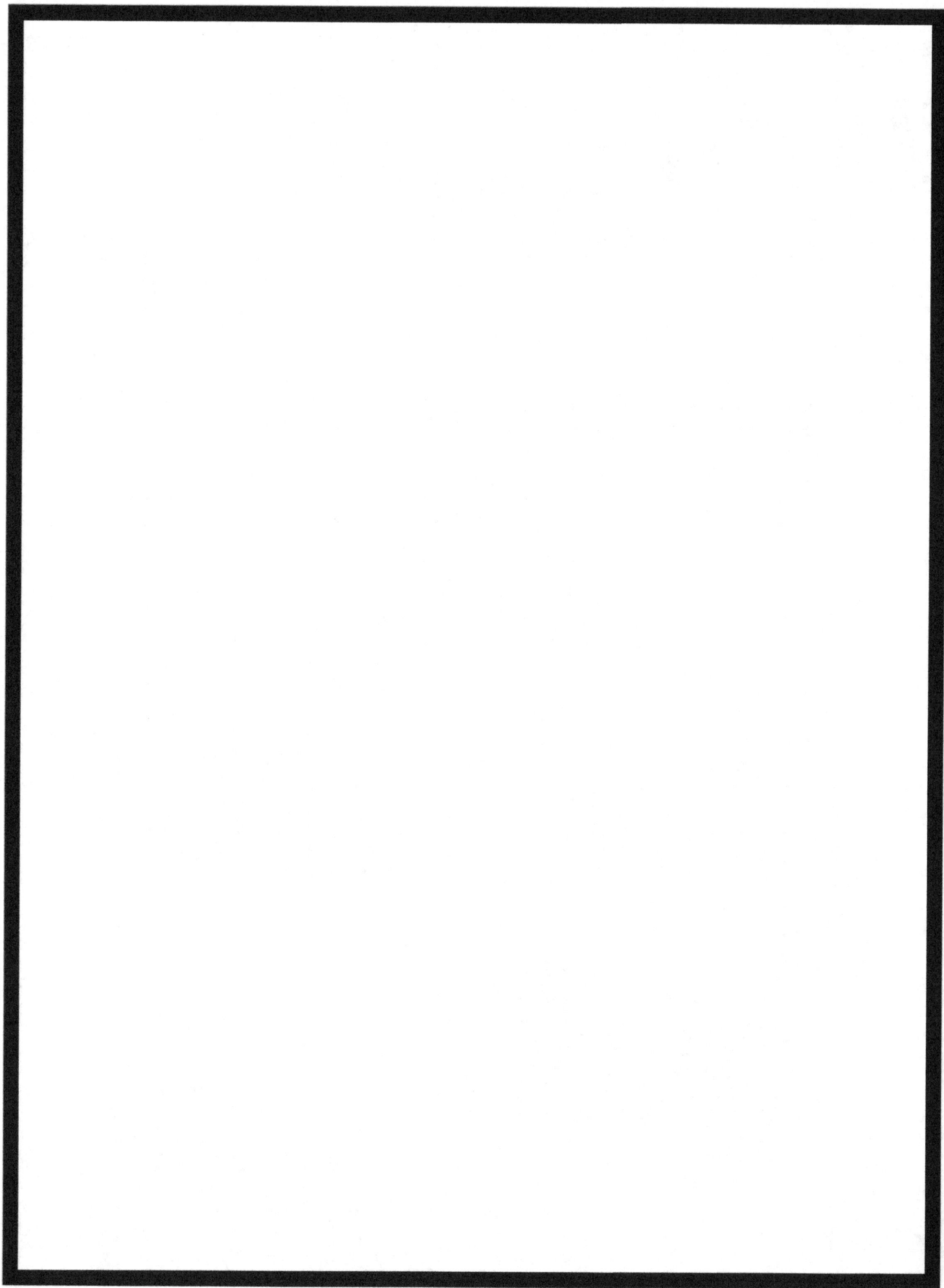

It's probably my age that tricks people into thinking I'm an adult

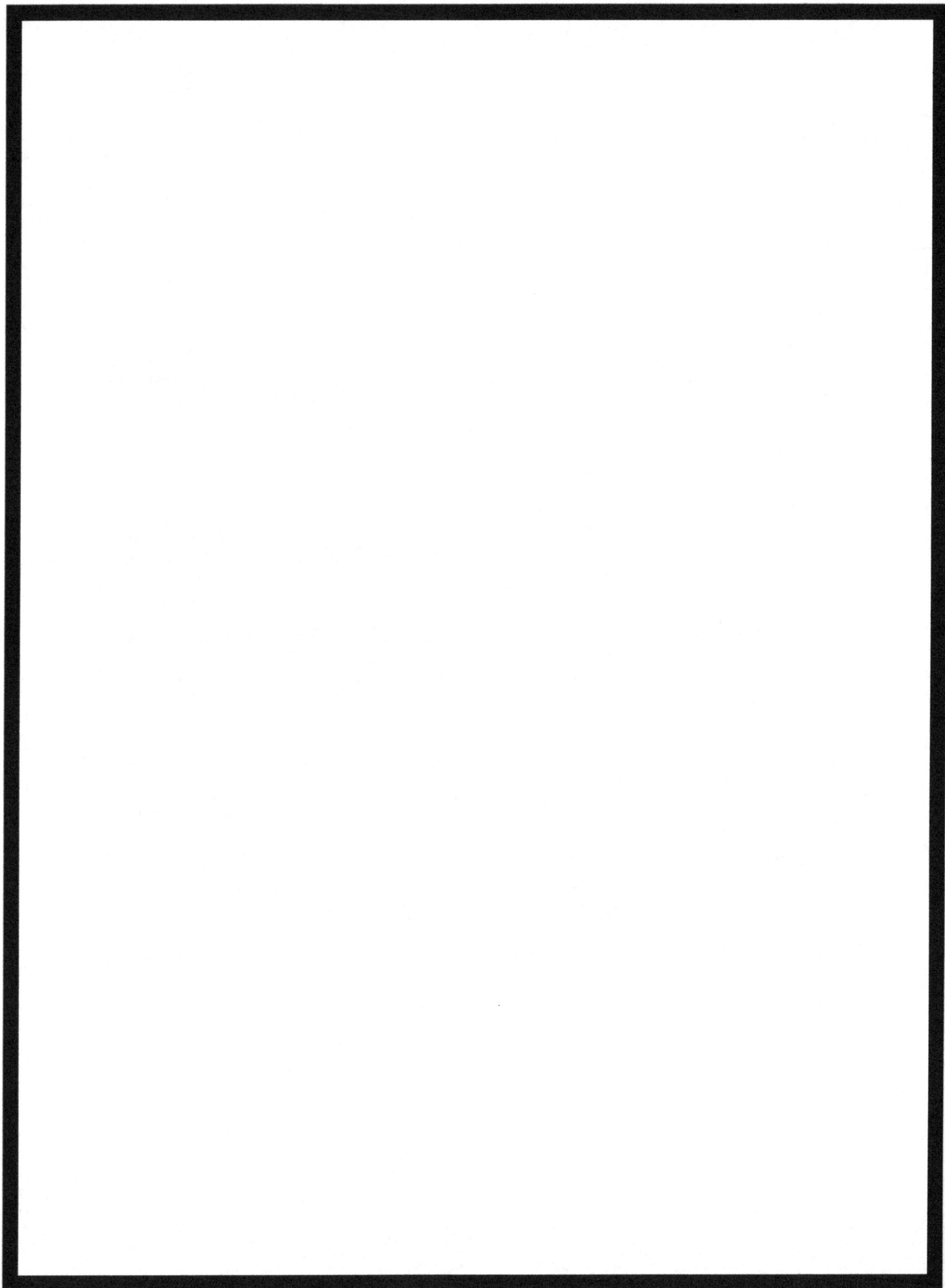

Two can keep a secret ..... if one is floating down the river

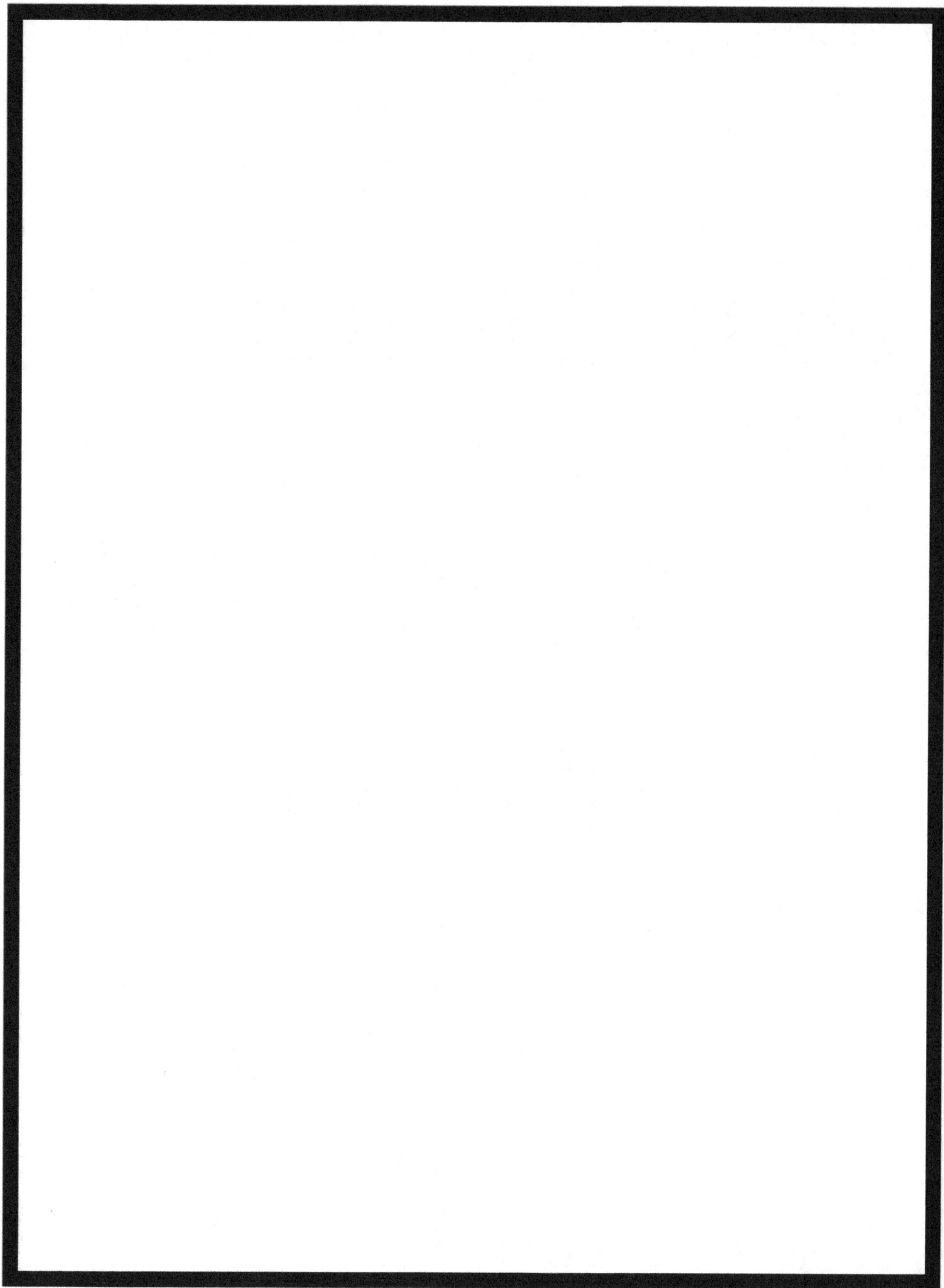

Once in a while I go outside and run the vacuum cleaner over the drive way just to ensure the neighbors never to talk to me

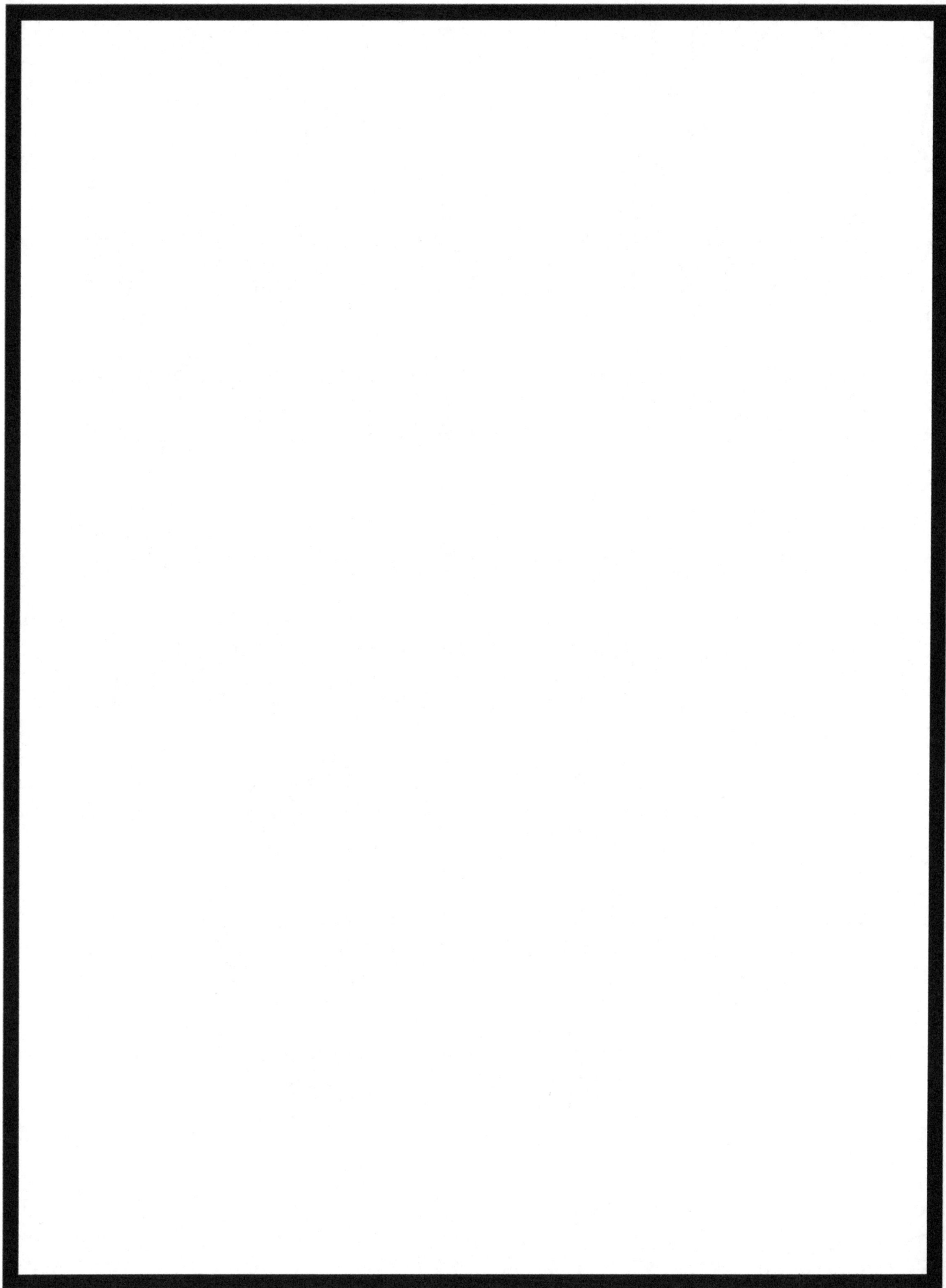

SOMETIMES THE FIRST STEP TOWARDS FORGIVENESS IS REALIZING THE OTHER PERSON IS AN IDIOT

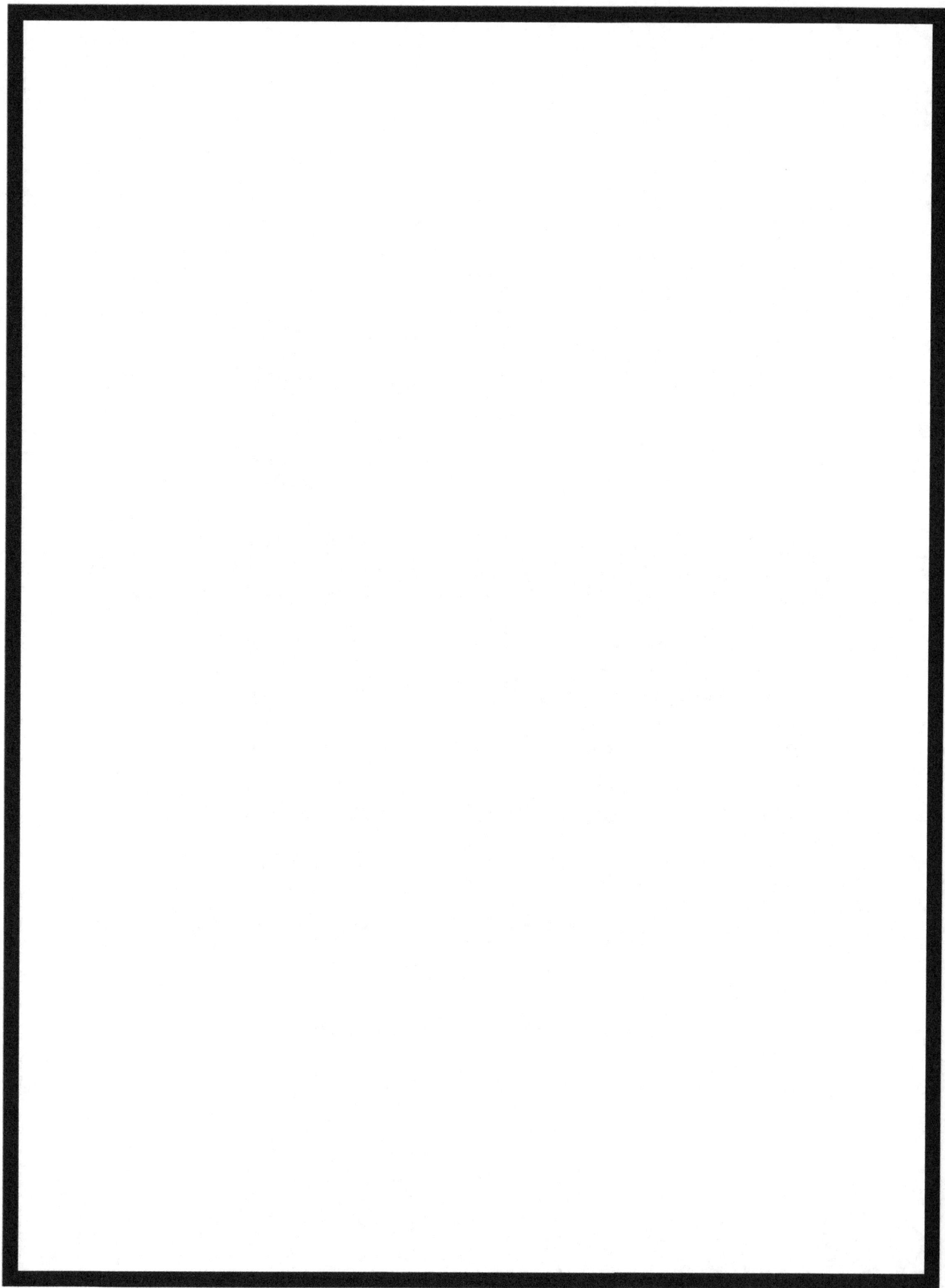

My level of sarcasm has gotten to the point where I don't even know if I'm kidding or not.

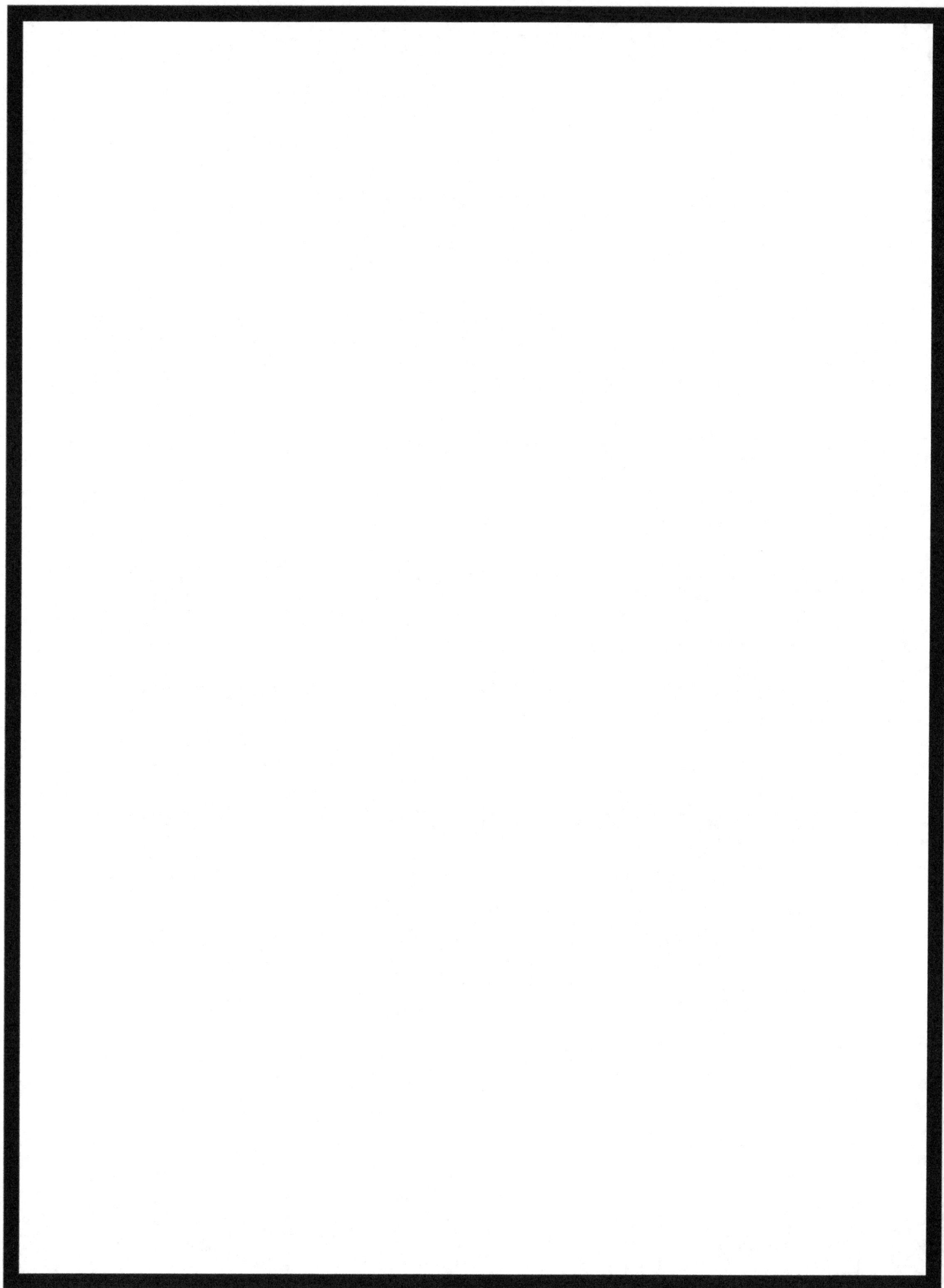

Made in the USA
Las Vegas, NV
28 February 2022